LIBRARY MANUALS

Volume 13

A PRIMER OF LIBRARIANSHIP

A PRIMER OF LIBRARIANSHIP

Edited by
W.E. DOUBLEDAY

LONDON AND NEW YORK

First published in 1931 by George Allen & Unwin Ltd

This edition first published in 2022
by Routledge
4 Park Square, Milton Park, Abingdon, Oxon OX14 4RN

and by Routledge
605 Third Avenue, New York, NY 10017

Routledge is an imprint of the Taylor & Francis Group, an informa business

Copyright © 1931 by Taylor & Francis.

All rights reserved. No part of this book may be reprinted or reproduced or utilised in any form or by any electronic, mechanical, or other means, now known or hereafter invented, including photocopying and recording, or in any information storage or retrieval system, without permission in writing from the publishers.

Trademark notice: Product or corporate names may be trademarks or registered trademarks, and are used only for identification and explanation without intent to infringe.

British Library Cataloguing in Publication Data
A catalogue record for this book is available from the British Library

ISBN: 978-1-03-213109-2 (Set)
ISBN: 978-1-00-322771-7 (Set) (ebk)
ISBN: 978-1-03-213115-3 (Volume 13) (hbk)
ISBN: 978-1-03-213119-1 (Volume 13) (pbk)
ISBN: 978-1-00-322775-5 (Volume 13) (ebk)

DOI: 10.4324/9781003227755

Publisher's Note
The publisher has gone to great lengths to ensure the quality of this reprint but points out that some imperfections in the original copies may be apparent.

Disclaimer
The publisher has made every effort to trace copyright holders and would welcome correspondence from those they have been unable to trace.

A PRIMER
OF LIBRARIANSHIP

BEING CHAPTERS OF PRACTICAL INSTRUCTION BY
RECOGNISED AUTHORITIES

Edited by

W E. DOUBLEDAY, Hon. F.L.A.

CHIEF LIBRARIAN OF THE HAMPSTEAD
PUBLIC LIBRARIES

LONDON
GEORGE ALLEN & UNWIN LTD
AND THE LIBRARY ASSOCIATION
1931

FIRST PUBLISHED IN 1931

All rights reserved
PRINTED IN GREAT BRITAIN BY
UNWIN BROTHERS LTD., WOKING

GENERAL INTRODUCTION TO THE SERIES

The publication of a systematic series of practical and authoritative Manuals of Library Work, which shall survey Library polity and practice in their latest aspects, is a requirement of which administrators, librarians, and students alike have long been conscious, and is much overdue.

In the Library world not the Great War alone, with its aftermath of new conditions, but also the Library Act of 1919, have marked the termination of one long epoch and the commencement of a new and yet more prosperous era. The removal of the crippling limitation of the penny rate at once paved the way for a renaissance of the Library Movement, and remarkable extensions and innovations, both in buildings and in service, have ensued. The great work of the Carnegie Trustees in fostering the development of urban Public Libraries has now been largely diverted into fresh channels, and County and Rural Library Systems now cover the country from Land's End to John-o'-Groats. The public demand and appreciation of Libraries have increased enormously, and, in response, old methods have been revised and new ones introduced. The evolution of Commercial and Technical Libraries and the development of Business and Works Libraries would amply suffice to indicate this spirit of progress, but, during the last decade or

A PRIMER OF LIBRARIANSHIP

so, the entire field of Library service has been subjected to review and experiment, and little, either in administration or routine, remains entirely unchanged.

It will, therefore, be sufficiently obvious that the old textbooks relating to Library practice can no longer serve, and that there is a real need for new manuals, written by persons of experience and authority, and treating of the new conditions in a full and thoroughly practical manner. It is this void that the series of Library Manuals is designed to fill, and the fact that these volumes are to be issued by Messrs. George Allen & Unwin Ltd. in conjunction with the Library Association, should afford adequate proof of the qualifications of the authors to treat of the subjects upon which they will write. If sufficient support is forthcoming the series will be made comprehensive and complete.

The volumes will be supplied with bibliographical references throughout, and will be illustrated where necessary. No effort will be spared to make the series an essential tool for all those who are engaged in Library work, or who intend to embrace Librarianship as a profession. To students they will be invaluable. The uniform price of 10s. 6d. net will be adhered to so far as possible, so as to bring the Manuals within the reach of all.

W. E. DOUBLEDAY
General Editor

PREFACE

The object of this Primer is to present a short survey of up-to-date librarianship in many of its more important aspects, with due regard to the most recent developments in municipal, university, commercial, and technical library practice.

The scope of the book has obviously dictated both selection and compression, but the range is wide, and several subjects which hitherto have escaped treatment in library manuals are included. Briefly, but in a practical manner, most of the curriculum of the courses of professional tuition is here considered. The contributions have been written by experts for the especial use of students and assistants, but it is hoped that the information will also form a useful conspectus for librarians and others who are interested in the rapidly extending Library Movement.

For more adequate treatment of the topics here dealt with readers are referred to the other volumes in the Library Association Series of Manuals, particulars of which may be found facing the title-page of this volume.

W. E. DOUBLEDAY

CONTENTS

CHAPTER		PAGE
	PREFACE	7
I.	BIBLIOGRAPHY by John Minto, M.A., F.L.A.	11
II.	BOOK SELECTION by J. E. Walker, F.L.A.	26
III.	BOOK CLASSIFICATION by Arthur J. Hawkes, F.L.A.	34
IV.	CATALOGUING by W. R. B. Prideaux, B.A., F.L.A.	45
V.	REFERENCE LIBRARIES by John Warner, F.L.A.	59
VI.	LENDING LIBRARIES by G. E. Roebuck, F.L.A.	70
VII.	LENDING LIBRARY ROUTINE WORK by Henry A. Sharp, F.L.A.	78
VIII.	AIDS TO READERS by R. D. Hilton Smith, F.L.A.	95
IX.	CHILDREN'S LIBRARY WORK by W. C. Berwick Sayers, F.L.A.	104
X.	COMMITTEE WORK AND OFFICE ROUTINE by Charles Nowell, F.L.A.	113
XI.	UNIVERSITY LIBRARIES by R. Offor, B.A., Ph.D., F.L.A.	127

A PRIMER OF LIBRARIANSHIP

CHAPTER		PAGE
XII.	LIBRARY EXTENSION WORK by Lionel R. McColvin, F.L.A.	138
XIII.	COUNTY LIBRARIES by Miss A. S. Cooke, A.L.A.	145
XIV.	LIBRARY CO-OPERATION AND THE NATIONAL CENTRAL LIBRARY by Luxmoore Newcombe, F.L.A.	153
XV.	COMMERCIAL AND TECHNICAL LIBRARIES by George Halsall	161
XVI.	BUSINESS LIBRARIES by B. M. Headicar, F.L.A.	174
XVII.	LIBRARY PUBLICATIONS by J. P. Lamb	183
XVIII.	PRINT COLLECTING by J. L. Douthwaite.	192
XIX.	BINDING FOR LIBRARIES by Douglas Cockerell	200
XX.	LIBRARY LAW by Alderman J. S. Pritchett, M.A., J.P.	208
XXI.	HOW TO ENTER THE LIBRARY PROFESSION by W. E. Doubleday, Hon. F.L.A.	213
	INDEX	221

A PRIMER OF LIBRARIANSHIP

CHAPTER I

BIBLIOGRAPHY

BY JOHN MINTO, M.A., F.L.A.
Librarian of the Signet Library, Edinburgh

The term Bibliography is used in two somewhat different senses. In the *Oxford English Dictionary* it is defined as "the systematic description and history of books, their authorship, printing, publication, editions, etc." In this sense it has to do with everything pertaining to the physical features and history of the book as a material object, and is not necessarily, or primarily, concerned with what the book may be about.

The bibliographic description of a book must include the title-page, the author's name in full, the place of printing, the printer's name, the date of printing, the size, the signatures, the number of leaves or pages, the collation (i.e. the number of sheets), the illustrations whether plain or coloured and the process employed (collotype, mezzotint, etc.), and any special peculiarity of binding or get-up which the book may display.

The first printers (who were also their own publishers and booksellers) had to compete in the market with the products of the scriptoria, the work of the clerks (*scribæ*) in the monasteries, who were the only disseminators of knowledge through the medium of books in manuscript. In order to compete with them successfully, the printer had to produce something which would make as good an appeal to the would-be purchaser as the beautiful MSS. which his rivals produced. To this end, in striking their founts of type, the early printers imitated as closely as possible the style of writing prevalent in the district where they set up their presses. They even copied the abbreviations which the scribes were accustomed to use; they frequently left blank spaces at the top left-hand corners of the first page and at the beginning of chapters, such as the writers of MSS. were wont to leave blank for illuminated initial letters. These blank initials were usually filled in by an illuminator after the printing was finished, but frequently were left blank altogether. Occasionally this blank space would have the initial letter to be illuminated printed in the centre of it for the guidance of the illuminator.

Many early printed books were issued without anything in the shape of a title-page, and the particulars which we now find there, known as the imprint, viz. printer's name, place and date of printing, were to be found at the end of the book in a paragraph, known as a colophon (a Greek word signifying the giving of the finishing touch to anything). The earliest known example of a printed title-page is dated 1463, but it was not until about 1480 that this became at all usual, and not until

BIBLIOGRAPHY

about 1530 that the provision of a title-page became part of the recognised make-up of a book. From that time the colophon gradually went out of use.

From the historical point of view, a systematic enumeration of the books of a special period is of importance as showing the subjects that occupied men's minds and activities at the period in question. For example, the catalogue of the great Thomason collection in the British Museum of Civil War, Commonwealth and Restoration pamphlets, books, newspapers, etc., provides a mirror of the times which, uncollected and uncatalogued, would be beyond the reach of the historian.

Why is this description of books, and the acquiring of the bibliographical knowledge which enables the description to be made, necessary for the librarian or the student of bibliography? If there were only one edition of every book, if books never became imperfect by being damaged, and never had to be replaced, minute description would not be necessary; but as there are many books and many editions of the same book, most of them differing in some particular, a statement of the differences in the various editions becomes of importance, and the detailed description of a perfect copy of a particular book becomes indispensable as a standard of reference.

There is, however, another sense in which the term "A Bibliography" is used, viz. "the systematic description of books on a particular subject." In this more restricted sense, the term is frequently applied to a list of books, articles in periodicals, special chapters in books, etc., dealing with the subject treated of, and appended or prefixed to a treatise on the subject. This form of bibliography is sometimes confined to a mere title-a-line list of works which the author has consulted, and as it gives few, if any, bibliographical particulars hardly deserves the term bibliography. A list of references would be a more correct designation.

Apart from these lists of references, the giving of which has of late come to be recognised as indispensable, there are innumerable subject bibliographies separately published. This class of bibliography is almost limitless, and may be compiled on any subject which has found literary form.

The bibliographer, however, may choose some special aspect of books other than their subject-matter on which to compile a bibliography. He may elect to deal with all books printed before a certain date, or in one country, or by one printer. He may confine himself to the works of one author or group of authors, to anonymous and pseudonymous books, privately printed or finely illustrated books, etc. In fact, there is no limit, as I have said, to the various forms which a bibliography may take.

Subject bibliographies are of the greatest importance, more particularly when their contents are arranged in chronological order. They are of value not only to the student but also to the future bibliographer as showing what work has already been done and what periods have been covered, so that

BIBLIOGRAPHY

he may avoid dealing with a subject already dealt with, or may supplement what has been published in his special field.

How, then, is the student of bibliography to obtain the necessary guidance in his study of the subject?

In *A Student's Manual of Bibliography*, by Arundell Esdaile, of the British Museum, Lecturer in Bibliography in the University of London School of Librarianship, recently published as the first of the series of Library Manuals, of which the present volume is one, the student will find an excellent guide to the art and science of bibliography from the pen of an expert. It covers all matters connected with the materials and methods of book production, the description of books, and the making of bibliographies. Examples of both primary and secondary classes of bibliographies are given, with a chapter on the arrangement of bibliographies. An appendix contains some examination questions, and samples of paper are inserted at the end of the volume.

A useful introduction to bibliography is the late H. G. Aldis's *The Printed Book*, which gives in a concise form information about the beginnings of printing, the spread of the art in the fifteenth and sixteenth centuries, and its development in England from 1500 to 1800. There are chapters on the construction of a book, the different methods of illustrating books, bookbinding and bookbindings, and how to handle books. A well selected bibliography is appended.

A PRIMER OF LIBRARIANSHIP

A most important text-book for students is R. B. McKerrow's *Introduction to Bibliography for Literary Students*, 1927. It is an expansion of his "Notes on Bibliographical Evidence for Literary Students and Editors of English Works of the 16th and 17th Centuries" (*Bibliog. Soc. Transac.*, v. 12). "The purpose of these notes," he says in his preface, "was to give to students of the literature of the period in which I was myself most interested, such elementary knowledge of the mechanical side of book production as might enable them to make better use than many of them seemed at the time able to do of the evidence as to a book's history which can be gathered from its material form and make-up." The rewritten and enlarged edition deals with English book production in general up to about the year 1800. It is concerned throughout with the problem of the relation of the printed book to the written word of the author and the processes involved in the transmission from MS. to printed book. A short list of some books of especial utility to students is prefixed.

C. T. Jacobi's *Some Notes on Books and Printing* is an excellent text-book, taking the student right through all the processes involved in the production of a book, beginning with the preparation of the MS. and the correction of proofs, followed by a chapter by F. Howard Collins on the making of an index. The types to be used, their names and sizes, the proper margins to be allowed in books of various sizes, the methods of illustration and the processes

BIBLIOGRAPHY

involved, printing papers and their sizes, the sizes of books, binding methods and what should be avoided therein, are next dealt with. Then follow chapters on publishing methods, agreements between author and publisher (specimens are given), and copyright. A glossary of bibliographical and typographical terms is added, with specimens of many types, and samples of various grades of paper.

It is desirable for the student of bibliography to have a knowledge of the material on which books are printed. This information can be obtained from R. W. Sindall's *The Manufacture of Paper*, which is an elementary well-illustrated text-book giving an outline of the various stages of manufacture and the materials used, such as cellulose, rags, esparto and straw, wood pulp, etc. There is a chapter on the deterioration of paper and a very full bibliography, covering both the technical and the historical side of paper-making.

In the matter of the illustration of books, *The British Museum Guide to the Processes and Schools of Engraving*, by Arthur M. Hind, is the best introduction to the subject. It deals in turn with the three forms of printing illustrations, relief, intaglio, and lithographic, detailing the processes of preparing the block, plate, or stone, and giving the history of each method. The processes dealt with are woodcut, wood engraving and relief prints from metal plates, line engraving, dry-point, etching, mezzotint, stipple, crayon, and the dot processes, aquatint, lithography, and colour printing. Miscellaneous notes on impressions, states, etc., are added, and a list of the technical terms occurring most frequently in the signatures and lettering on prints.

In regard to bookbinding, Douglas Cockerell's *Some Notes on Bookbinding* is recommended as an introductory study. It is based on demonstration lectures which he gave at the London County Council School of Arts and Crafts to students of the School of Librarianship, University College, London. It contains all that the budding librarian needs to know about bookbinding and its methods, which are all made very clear by the fine illustrations from line drawings by Miss Doris Meyer.

The same author's *Bookbinding and the Care of Books* is a fuller and more technical text-book, in which all the processes are set out in detail with drawings and other illustrations. It contains valuable chapters on the injurious influences to which books are liable to be subjected, methods of preserving old bindings, and rebacking. Detailed specifications, in accordance with the Society of Arts special report, are given for four different sizes and classes of books according to the use to which they are to be put. A glossary of terms and reproductions of fine bindings are added.

The *Manual of Library Bookbinding*, by Henry T. Coutts and George A. Stephen, deals with both the practical and the historical aspects of binding, and gives a succinct account of the processes of modern binding, describing the methods of both hand and machine binding. It describes, and gives actual

BIBLIOGRAPHY

examples of, materials for library binding, the different methods of recording and checking books sent to the binder; gives practical advice as to the setting-up of binderies in libraries, on the repairing of books, recipes for treatment of binding, and a list of authorities on book preservation. A glossary of terms completes a very practical treatise.

In addition to the above-mentioned text-books there are several reference books which the student should make himself familiar with.

Mr. Arundell Esdaile's Sandars lectures on *The Sources of English Literature* make an excellent bibliography in narrative form indicating the methods to be adopted and the sources to be examined in compiling a complete bibliography of the literature of our own country.

The Bookman's Glossary, by John A. Holden, is a dictionary of terms and proper names used in the bookselling and allied trades, giving examples of various kinds of type-faces, a list of proof-readers' marks, and miscellaneous information.

C. T. Jacobi's *Printing* is a practical treatise on the art of typography as applied more particularly to the printing of books. There is a chapter on methods of book-illustration and the papers set for the written examinations of the City and Guilds of London Institute from 1917–19, and the questions in knowledge of printing, 1909–14, set for the examinations for clerks in H.M. Stationery Office.

The Society of Arts *Report of the Committee on Leather for Bookbinding* is a most valuable reference book. The Sub-Committee of experts visited a number of important libraries with a view to ascertaining the causes of the deterioration of leather bindings, and by comparing bindings of different times, by observing conditions of ventilation, lighting, heating, etc., in different libraries to note the effect of environment on the durability of the leather, the relative suitability of various leathers, and to find out how far faulty construction is responsible for want of durability in modern leather bindings. A specification is given for the binding of heavy and valuable books and a suggested specification for ordinary library binding. Both specifications are illustrated to show methods. There are numerous coloured plates showing deterioration to various leathers, tanned with different materials, after exposure to light and air and gas fumes for various periods.

NOTES ON BIBLIOGRAPHICAL AND TYPOGRAPHICAL TERMS

BASTARD TITLE. See HALF-TITLE.

BLOCK BOOKS. Books printed from wooden blocks on which the lettering to be printed has been cut out in relief as in a woodcut.

BROADSIDE or BROADSHEET. A page of letterpress printed on one side only, e.g. proclamations, bills, etc., meant to be posted up.

CANCEL. Any part of a book substituted for what was originally printed.

CAPTION. The heading at the beginning of the text, or of a chapter, section, etc.

BIBLIOGRAPHY

Case. A shallow tray, divided into compartments or "boxes," each containing a different type letter, and so arranged that the most commonly used letters are near the compositor's hand. Cases are used in pairs set up on a sloping stand, the "upper case" resting on the top edge of the "lower case," and placed at a more upright angle. The upper case contains the capital letters, numerals, accented letters, and various characters; the lower case contains the ordinary letters, spaces, etc.

Catchwords. The first word, or part of a word, of the following page printed in a separate line at the foot (right-hand corner) of a page, probably as a guide to the printer in imposition. The earliest printed books had no catchwords, which began to be used about 1471. They perform the same function as signatures.

Chain Lines and Wire Lines. These are the faint semi-transparent lines seen on paper when a page is held up to the light. The horizontal lines, which are more widely spaced, are known as chain lines, the vertical lines as wire lines. They are caused by the wire bed of the mould in which the paper is made.

Chase. A metal frame in which pages of type for printing are placed and tightly "locked-up" with quoins or "furniture."

Collation.—One is said to collate a book when by checking the proper sequence of the signatures one ascertains whether the book is complete or not.

Supposing a book to consist of 4 preliminary leaves unsigned, comprising half-title, title-page, and 2 leaves of preface, 4 leaves of contents, etc., signed b, followed by the text in 22 gatherings or sheets, of 4 leaves each, signed by the capital letters from B to Z (except J, U, and W, which are usually omitted) and 23 gatherings signed Aa to Zz, the bibliographical collation would be expressed thus: [A]^4, b^4, B–Z^4, Aa–Zz^4. The superior or index figures indicate the number of leaves in a gathering. The preliminary matter, which is usually without signatures, is treated as having the signature A.

Colophon. A statement at the end of a book giving the title, author's and printer's or publisher's name, date and place of printing. All of these items are not always given: one or more may be omitted. The printer's or publisher's device may be added.

Edition. The whole number of copies of a book printed at any time or times from one setting up of type (including copies printed from stereotypes or electrotypes made from that setting).

Impression. The whole number of copies printed at one time, usually without removing the type from the machine.

Issue. Some special form of the book in which for the most part the original printed sheets are used, but which differs from the earlier or normal form by the addition of new matter or by some difference in arrangement.

Factotum. An ornamental block with a space in the centre in which an initial capital letter may be printed is called a factotum initial, or simply factotum.

Format. The form, size, shape, and general get-up of a book.

In a *Folio* (Fol., 2°), the sheets are folded once, making 2 leaves (4 pages). In a *Quarto* (4to, 4°), they are folded twice, making 4 leaves (8 pages). In an *Octavo* (8vo or 8°), they are folded thrice, making 8 leaves (16 pages).

Forme. The pages of type arranged in a chase in proper order for printing.

Foul Case. In distributing type after printing, the compositor may occasionally drop a letter into the wrong box or division of the case, or it may happen if a box is filled to overflowing with type letters, some of

BIBLIOGRAPHY

these may slip down into the box underneath, causing foul case.

FOUNT. The whole assortment of letters of the same style or "face" and size of body.

FRISKET. A light frame attached by a hinge to the free end of the tympan (*q.v.*) in such a way that it can be folded down between the tympan and the forme. It is covered with a sheet of paper in which holes are cut corresponding to the pages of type to allow the type to print.

FURNITURE. Wooden or metal fittings used for making margins or (like quoins) for packing type as set in chases.

GALLEY. A shallow tray with edges on three sides somewhat lower than the height of the type, in which the compositor places the lines of type which he has set up from his composing stick when it is full. When the galley is filled, the type is inked with a roller, and a strip of paper somewhat wider than the galley is placed on it, and a print or "pull" is taken, known as a *galley proof*, for correction. When corrected, sufficient type to make up a page, or pages, is tied up with string to keep it together, and placed in a forme to be made ready for printing.

HALF-TITLE. A brief title, usually without author's name or imprint printed, on a leaf preceding the title-page proper: called also bastard title.

HEADLINE. A line of type at the top of a page above the text indicating the contents of the page. When the line consists of the title of the book, it is called a running title or running head.

HEADPIECE. An ornamental design at the top of a page is called a head ornament or headpiece. A similar ornament at the foot of the matter in a page is called a tailpiece.

IMPOSITION. When the number of pages required to make a sheet has been completed, the printer "imposes" them on a flat table or stone in such a way that after printing the pages will be in their proper order when the paper is folded.

IMPRESSION. See under EDITION.

IMPRIMATUR, i.e. Let it be printed. The term used in authorising the printing of a book by the press censor or licenser.

IMPRINT. The lower part of the title-page giving the place of printing, printer's or publisher's name, and date.

ISSUE. See under EDITION.

JUSTIFICATION. The filling out of the lines of type to an even length of metal.

LEADING. When a strip of type metal is placed between lines of type to show a blank space, the type is said to be "leaded."

LINOTYPE. A modern method of casting type in "slugs" or lines by means of a composing machine, molten metal being directed into matrices by keyboard action.

MARGINS. The blank edges of the printed page known as the inner, head, outer and tail margins, usually varying in size in the order given, from the inner (the narrowest) to the tail (the widest).

MONOTYPE. Somewhat similar to Linotype, but in this case the letters remain as separate entities.

PLATEN (Old form). A thick piece of beechen board reinforced with an iron plate which, when brought down on the type by means of a screw, presses the paper on the type, and so gives the impression.

PLATEN (Modern use). A small machine for printing with a flat surface, not rotary, employed chiefly for proofs and jobbing work; may be operated by foot or mechanical power.

POINT SYSTEM (Typographical). A numerical method of indicating sizes of type in accordance with the thickness of their "body," which has almost entirely superseded the old system of individual type-names. Higher

BIBLIOGRAPHY

numbers denote larger types: thus the old Brevier is known as 8-point, and Pica as 12-point bodies.

QUADS. Pieces of metal lower than the type, similar to spaces but much broader, used for filling out the blank ends of lines.

QUOINS. Wedges of wood or metal used in locking up a chase.

RECTO and VERSO. The right-hand and left-hand page, respectively, of an opened book.

REGISTER. A list of the gatherings or signatures given at the end of the book as a guide to the binder.

In letterpress printing, perfect "register" is obtained when the printing on one side of the paper backs exactly upon the printing on the other.

REGLETS. Strips of wood used as leads in place of the ordinary type-metal ones.

RUNNING TITLE. The title of a book printed in a line at the top of every page above the letterpress.

SHEET. The group or "gathering" of leaves between the middle pair of which the thread with which the book is sewn is passed by the binder.

SIGNATURE. The letter, figure, or other mark, printed at the foot of the first page of each sheet to guide the binder in arranging the sheets in correct order.

TYMPAN. An iron frame covered with a sheet of parchment or thick paper and hinged to the wooden frame enclosing the bed of the press in such a way that it can be turned back to have the paper about to be printed laid upon it. When this has been done, it is turned over and brought down upon the type for an impression to be taken.

VERSO. See RECTO.

WATERMARK. A design or name showing in semi-transparency when the paper is held up to the light. It is the paper-maker's trade mark.

WIRE LINES. See CHAIN LINES.

CHAPTER II

BOOK SELECTION

BY J. E. WALKER, F.L.A.
Chief Librarian, Public Library, Hendon.

Book selection is as important as it is probably the most interesting part of the work of a librarian. Without care it can become the easiest way of wasting the scanty funds of a library, so that infinite pains should be taken to ensure that the comparatively few books that can be bought out of the many that exist are the "best" for that particular library, otherwise the rash buyer will soon fall a prey to every variety of book agent that dogs his footsteps.

The principles of selection are the same for every library, though the results will vary according to its objects. If the great national libraries, which obtain their books mainly from the operation of the Copyright Act, and possibly also the specialist library that collects everything in its limited field, are excluded, most others have to employ selection to secure their additions from the many thousands of works that are published annually. In the small library this process becomes a selection within a selection.

The printed aids used are (i) the general book selection guides; (ii) the special book selection guides; and (iii) articles and reviews in literary and other book reviewing journals. There is also a

BOOK SELECTION

further "aid," namely, the requests of readers expressed at the point of service.

Examples of the first are Sonnenschein's *Best Books*; Nelson's *Standard Books*, now sadly in need of revision; and the *Catalogue of British Scientific and Technical Books* published by the British Science Guild. The last named is included in this group because its editors have used the term "scientific" in its broadest sense, making it more general than special. In the second class are included the guides to historical fiction by Baker and Nield; Davies' *Bibliography of British History Stuart Period*, 1603–1714; the useful reading lists issued by the Historical Association; lists contained in the *Sessional Programme* of the Department of Technology of the City and Guilds of London Institute; and the excellent "What to Read" handbooks written by experts and published by the Leeds Public Libraries Committee. For the third it is only necessary to name *The Times Literary Supplement* and the *Geographical Journal* as respectively representing general and special periodicals.

Printed guides in book form can usually be divided into two classes, namely, the select and the comprehensive. The former is of most use to the book selector, especially if it is graded and annotated.

It is to printed guides that the librarian must turn for the selection of books for a new library, but before he does anything with them he should decide how many books can be bought for the

TABLE OF INITIAL STOCK

Description	Lending		Reference		Total	
	Volumes	Percentage of Stock	Volumes	Percentage of Stock	Volumes	Percentage of Stock
General Works	56	0·24	493	10·97	549	2·0
Philosophy	479	2·07	53	1·17	532	1·9
Religion	631	2·73	238	5·3	869	3·2
Sociology	1,147	4·96	377	8·4	1,524	5·5
Language	166	0·72	155	3·5	321	1·2
Science	1,183	5·13	327	7·3	1,510	5·5
Useful Arts	1,215	5·26	351	7·8	1,566	5·7
Fine Arts	1,669	7·23	449	10·0	2,118	7·6
Literature	3,330	14·43	609	13·56	3,939	14·2
History, Biography, Topography	3,867	16·74	1,440	32·0	5,307	19·2
Fiction	9,353	40·49	—	—	9,353	34·0
Total	23,096	100·0	4,492	100·0	27,588	100·0

BOOK SELECTION

money available, and roughly how they should be divided among the several classes of literature.

As so many published statistics relate to old libraries, the table on page 28 may be of interest, for it gives the numbers and percentages of volumes in each class, excluding children's books, of the initial stock of a new library in a district with a population of about 100,000 in the London area. It is to be noted in this statement that there is a higher percentage of fiction than is given in similar tables elsewhere. This is to be expected in a new library where there is a maximum demand for novels almost from the beginning.

So far as the actual selection of books for an initial stock is concerned, probably the best method is to take one of the general guides, say Sonnenschein, and go through it page by page, entering on a 5×3 card particulars of each book noted. By frequent reference to the subjects scheduled in any good modern scheme of book classification the selector will guard against any important subject being overlooked. He should further supplement his researches in Sonnenschein by referring to the various special guides and thus provide against the omission of important books.

This done, and the record of any book inadvertently duplicated erased, it remains for the cards to be arranged in broad classes. Book lists may then be typed, submitted to the responsible committee, if such is the established custom, and then sent to the bookseller.

A method recommended is to send the lists to second-hand booksellers before ordering any new books. In this way it is possible to get reports from places far apart, a more satisfactory and less time-wasting practice than to rely solely upon personal search through booksellers' catalogues or visits to shops. Moreover, the lists reach those who do not issue a catalogue. In this connection *Book Auction Records* will be found a useful tool when the prices quoted for old books appear to be too high. It is no part of the duty of the selector for a popular library to pay high prices for out-of-print books: first editions and similar items should be left to the private collector.

Once the library is established as a going concern, it will be found that the greater part of its annual additions will be of current publications. For their selection reviews in periodicals will be used, though at no time in its existence can the printed bibliography be dispensed with. No library has ever found it possible to buy every desirable book when its nucleus stock was being assembled, and gaps can only be filled gradually over a long period.

Can the review be relied upon for the selection of books? The question is one that has often been debated, and the answer, so far as the best journals are concerned, must be in the affirmative. And it is only to the best that the librarian should resort for guidance. Most good books are noticed if they are sent to editors for that purpose, but limitations of space will allow long reviews only to the few.

BOOK SELECTION

Because of defects (from the book selection point of view) in many reviews, personal examination by the librarian is sometimes advocated as being the best method of selection. It would be so if he were an authority on the subject, but in many cases it is unsatisfactory for the layman to decide whether a book, otherwise attractive, is accurate in fact and statement, and therefore a desirable purchase. If it has any blemish it will probably be noted in periodicals of good standing. This is not to say that a book should be bought only on the strength of a long and laudatory review, especially in a specialist magazine. One of many pages written by an authority in such a paper as *Mind*, or the *Hibbert Journal*, while indicating the importance of the book and its high place in the literature of philosophy or religion, would not prove that it would find sufficient local readers to justify its purchase. After all, the existence of readers interested in the subject must be a first consideration.

The expert, if given a free hand, could very easily fill the library shelves with erudite treatises that might not circulate from one year's end to another; they would doubtless be good books, but not for that particular library. For such demands the National Central Library exists, and it would be wasteful to lock up money in their purchase when it could otherwise be usefully employed. The selector's task, first and last, is to obtain the best books on all subjects that appeal to his readers, and to keep each section as up to date as possible within the limits of the sum of money available.

Readers' recommendations are a valuable aid in assembling a collection that will reflect the expressed wants of borrowers, for they tend to show the kind of book that is in local demand, and reveal gaps in the stock that might otherwise escape notice. Most library committees welcome these suggestions as providing tangible proof of the interest that is being taken in their library. Suggestions are usually made in a book provided for the purpose, or on cards of the same size as those on which the titles selected by the librarian himself are entered, and with them they can be filed. Persons making the recommendations should be required to give as much bibliographical information about the book as possible. In addition to essential particulars regarding author, title, publisher, price, etc., it is desirable that references to or quotations from reviews should be made.

If all suggestions are examined at least once a week, an early decision can be made as to whether the book is to be put on the next list for Committee, or whether it is one which should more properly be obtained from the National Central Library. If the latter, the borrower can be informed at once; if the former, he should be told of the Committee's decision, and, if favourable, advised that the book will be reserved for him as soon as it is ready for circulation. By dealing with these matters promptly and letting the reader know the fate of his suggestions, even if they are turned down, there will be built up a reputation for courtesy and efficiency that will more than repay the little extra work involved.

BOOK SELECTION

Personal enquiries made of the staff should always be noted on paper, otherwise they might be forgotten. An "enquiries" book kept at the counter has been found useful as a record of what readers are searching for either in the way of specific books or subjects. A ruling for such a book suggests itself, but there should be a column for noting whether or not a borrower is willing to pay postage if the book can be obtained from another library. By this means the urgency of the need can be tested and decision helped as to whether the book should be borrowed or bought or whether no action should be taken. The wants of diffident readers unwilling to make suggestions in a more formal manner can often be satisfied in this way, and the library will thereby add materially to the service it gives its public.

If each member of a staff can be brought to take an active and intelligent interest in this work of selection and of building up a well balanced collection, the whole process should function as smoothly and efficiently as a machine, and through the library there will constantly flow "a stream of living books."

CHAPTER III

BOOK CLASSIFICATION

BY ARTHUR J. HAWKES, F.L.A.
Borough Librarian of the Public Library, Wigan

Book classification is the organisation of knowledge contained in a collection of books. Books may be *arranged* according to various systems (by size, by authors, or by subject alphabetically, either as a whole collection or in several large departments); but libraries are not said to be *classified* unless the books are arranged in a complete systematic order according to the accepted principles of logical classification.

Whilst it is commonly stated that a book classification is the same as a knowledge classification with such modifications as are necessitated by the physical form of books, this is far from being the fact, except in so far that all classifications are classifications of knowledge. Every classification designed for a special purpose classifies some section of knowledge or the objects of knowledge. Classifications are distinguished from one another by the purpose the classifier has in view. Some classifications are only sectional, others are general, that is they embrace the whole field of knowledge. Even general classifications may differ widely from one another, according as the interest and purpose of the classifier differs, yet all may be perfectly sound classifications, conforming to the accepted canons of logical classification.

Each different purpose or plan is called the *characteristic* of the classification. Thus an anthropologist might construct a general classification to serve his special purpose in which the ethnological interest of the objects classified was the chief consideration. His classification would thus have an *ethnological characteristic*. A geographer making a general classification might make geographical distribution his characteristic. A philosopher would aim to display the cosmical relationships of the objects classified. Sectional classifications might differ in precisely the same way. A musical instrument maker, a metallurgist, and a chemist might all make classifications of metals with very different results. Each would choose a characteristic which suited his purpose. Yet, provided the characteristic chosen is capable of universal application within the limits of the group of objects classified, the resulting scheme would be perfectly legitimate; and each would be a classification of knowledge.

Consequently, to say that a book classification is a classification of knowledge does not help us very much to solve the problems involved in classifying books. What we have to do is to determine the true characteristic of a practically useful book classification. What this is depends upon the nature of our material (books) and what we seek to achieve. It is too big a subject to discuss here with any fullness, but we shall consider it briefly a little later on. For the moment we will deal with the logical aspects of the matter.

The Characteristic of a classification must be essential to its purpose, and, in the case of general classifications, capable of universal application. Any principle of universal application may be made the basis of a sound and natural system of classification, though two such classifications may be widely different. A classification is only a good classification in so far as it serves the purpose in hand. No matter how strictly a classifier may adhere to the laws of logic, if his classification fails to demonstrate what he aims to display or fails to achieve the purpose he has in hand it is a bad classification.

Having decided upon his characteristic the classifier must proceed with the work of grouping and subdivision strictly according to the logical laws of classification. He has a choice of two methods in commencing his task. He may begin by assembling together all the objects he wishes to classify and, by choosing some point of difference, divide them into two groups. These two groups he may again subdivide in the same way and may continue subdividing the resulting groups into smaller groups until he has reduced them to the compass he desires. This is known as the *bifurcate* method of classification, and an analysis of the method may be used to demonstrate all the logical principles of classification.

The most elementary example of the process is the famous *Tree of Porphyry*. Porphyry divided universal SUBSTANCE into Corporeal and Incorporeal substance. Corporeal substance or BODY he divided into Animate and Inanimate body. Animate body or LIVING BEING he divided into Sensible and Insensible living being. Sensible living being or ANIMAL he divided into Rational (Man) and Irrational Animal. To "Substance" he is said to have added the *difference* "corporeality" and derived body. The "Difference" is the quality exhibited by a portion of one group (called the *genus*) by which a smaller group (called the *species*) is marked off. Similarly, if the genus we are proposing to divide is Timbers we might add the difference "hardness" and mark off the species Hard-Timbers.

A genus may be a species of a larger group, whilst a species may be a genus to a smaller group. In Porphyry's tree Animal is a species to Living Being, but a genus to the lesser group Man. When the series is a long one the lower groups are frequently called *subaltern species*. The first or original group of a series is termed the *Summum Genus*; the lowest species is termed the *Infima Species*.

This process, as elaborated by Porphyry, well illustrates the primary law: that classification must proceed from terms of considerable extension and limited intension to terms of limited extension and great intension. "Substance" is a term of great extension because it compasses everything in the universe. It is said to have little intension because it has very few qualities. At the other end of the series "Man" is a term of much less extension because it denotes many less objects; it has much greater intension, however, because Man is an object expressing innumerable qualities: his form, organisation, senses, reason, and so forth. Always, the final groups of a classified series are intensive, whilst the initial groups are extensive.

The Differences chosen to mark off the groups must be real differences, not casual or accidental differences. That is to say, the qualities chosen as "Differences" must be qualities which have a relation to the characteristic of the classification. Thus if we are making a biological classification of the animal kingdom, the qualities chosen to differentiate the genera and species must be anatomical and fundamental qualities. Qualities such as skin-colour or tractability would be accidental qualities and useless for our purpose. *Accident* is defined in logic as "any quality which may indifferently belong or not belong to a class or group without affecting the other qualities of the class." On the other hand, qualities which may be regarded as accidental according to one characteristic of classification may be real qualities under another characteristic. If we are classifying animals from the point of view of their usefulness to man tractability might be regarded as an important quality. Classifications based on real differences are called *Natural Classifications*; those based upon accidental differences are called *Artificial Classifications*. Whilst artificial classifications serve some purposes, they are extremely limited, and subdivision cannot be continued

BOOK CLASSIFICATION

beyond two or three stages. Cross-division and chaos rapidly result.

If we start our classification with a number of initial groups or classes, instead of commencing from unity as by the bifurcate method, we must make certain that our initial groups cover all knowledge within the limits of our scheme. For instance, in making a classification scheme for Bookbinding we might start by setting up the following main classes:—BOOKBINDING: Materials; Technology; Organisation. How can we be sure that these groups will accommodate all our material? A very simple test is to correspond them to terms of Porphyry's tree. Thus

Bookbinding	= Substance
Materials	= Body
Technology	= Life
(Machinery and Processes)	
Organisation	= Mind.

By this simple test we not only check our compass, but obtain a guide as to the true content of each division.

What constitutes the characteristic of a good book classification depends entirely upon what we desire to achieve by it, and the nature of books themselves. Books generally are of two kinds: those which supply information or expound theories, etc., and those which are in the nature of literary art, imaginative literature, and *belles-lettres*. In the main the books in the first category aim to help men and women in the vocations and avocations of life. It is very important to realise this because in general the association of two or more allied topics in one book is generally due to a corresponding association in the practical affairs of life—not because the topics themselves are intrinsically allied by their physical nature. For instance, Jewellery and precious stones are often dealt with together, though in a philosophical scheme of classification the topics are widely separated. Similarly, the intrinsically different crafts of Pattern-making and Cast-iron work are definitely conjoined, whilst furniture and pottery, printing and paper-making are frequently associated.

By contrast let us quote a section from a philosophical scheme designed as a classification for books:—

>   Architecture—
>   Plans
>   Sites
>   Elevation
>   Construction
>   Materials
>   Bricks
>   Brick-making
>   Kilns, etc.
>   Other materials
>   Architectural details
>   Architectural styles.

Now, whilst *philosophically* much can be said for associating Building Construction with Architecture, Bricks with Building Construction, and Kilns with Bricks, such associations have no relation to *Book Classification*; it is safe to say that no book in existence associates those subjects between two covers, for the simple reason that the profession of architecture, the craft of building, and the art of brickmaking are, in practical life, different vocations, and books as a whole reflect these vocational differences. On the other hand, architectural elevation, architectural styles, and architectural details are certainly found together in any text-book of architecture. Yet in the above classification scheme they are widely separated. This well illustrates the fundamental difference between what is properly called a knowledge classification and a book classification. The association of subjects in book classification must correspond to the actual association of the same subjects in the books themselves. Our business is the classification of books not ideas. Consequently, *the characteristic of book classification is human vocation or avocation*, and the nearer our associations of topics in the classification correspond to the vocational relationships of life, the more helpful will our classified libraries be to the seekers after information.

In this way we shall certainly succeed in achieving Dr. Richardson's ideal of book classification—that of "having the most-used-books together in the classes in which they are used together." It will also meet Mr. Wyndham Hulme's view that book classification is "a mechanical time-saving operation for the discovery of knowledge in literature."

Even the classification of imaginative literature can be adapted to this characteristic, for the vocation in this instance is the vocation of the student, and the way these classes are grouped or subdivided for the purposes of academic study is the way they should be classified in libraries where students resort. The Library of Congress Classification which divides imaginative literature first by language and then by period, disregarding form, most nearly meets this requirement. In special cases, such as the Elizabethan period, there is a further subdivision by "form" because student practice demands it. Elizabethan drama is an important subject of itself, but is more often studied in relation to Elizabethan poetry than in relation, say, to Victorian drama.

To the people, however, the reading of imaginative literature is a recreation, an avocation, consequently in popular libraries the classification of these books is quite properly by language and then by form. "Form," of course, means the form in which the book is cast—the verse form, the drama form, and the novel form.

Many of the alleged difficulties of book classification disappear if the vocational characteristic is kept consistently in mind. Nevertheless, there will always be traps for the unwary. The greatest cause of "howlers" in classification is *confounding the matter of a book with its subject*. Titles must not be taken at their face value, for frequently they are more poetic than practical. Such a case is Ruskin's *Notes on the Construction of Sheepfolds*, which is a treatise on Church discipline. On the other hand, the

BOOK CLASSIFICATION

matter of a book is equally often a false guide to its true subject. A book on the Mendelian doctrine of heredity may be wholly concerned with sweet peas, primroses, or pigs, yet the subject of the book is heredity. Primroses or pigs are merely the vehicles of research. In these cases the titles of the books are a better guide to the true subject than the tables of contents. All books must be examined as a whole, title and contents, in relation to the author's purpose.

Another difficulty which besets the classifier is the twin-subject title: *The Flora of Hampshire, Bookkeeping for Ironmongers, The Portraits of Mary Queen of Scots.* Where should such books be placed—with Botany or with Hampshire, with Book-keeping or with Ironmongery, with Portraiture or with Biography? Such books must be classified with the subject which has the greater *comparative value.* That is to say, the classifier must consider which student will be helped most by being able to compare one book with an allied book. Is the person interested in the topography or the history of Hampshire more likely to be benefited by having the botany of the county at his elbow, or the student of British flora? Clearly the latter. Similarly with Book-keeping. The book-keeper may have to change his job at any moment—from being a butcher's accountant he may become an ironmonger's accountant. It is the professional book-keeper who most frequently requires books on special phases of this subject and they should be placed where they have the greatest comparative value. The ironmonger who does his own book-keeping at least knows that the subject he requires belongs to a distinct profession, and it is most unlikely that he would expect to find such a work in the ironmongery section. On the other hand, the portraits of Queen Mary are personal in the extreme and are better placed with other books relating to her life.

CHAPTER IV

CATALOGUING

BY W. R. B. PRIDEAUX, B.A., F.L.A.
Librarian of the Reform Club, London

To make a catalogue of a library is not the same thing as to make a list of the books in the library, such as a shelf-list or accessions register. A catalogue is distinguished from a mere list or enumeration "by systematic or methodical arrangement, alphabetical or other order, and often by the addition of brief particulars, descriptive or aiding identification, indicative of locality, position, date, price, or the like" (*N.E.D.*). In so far as cataloguing deals with the description of books, it is a branch of bibliography, which has been defined as "the systematic description and history of books" (*N.E.D.*)

The objects of a catalogue are to give sufficient details about a book to identify it, and sometimes to give additional helpful bibliographical or other information, with any necessary particulars about the actual copy in the library; to show if a given book is in the library; and to indicate what books by a given author, on a given subject, or in a given kind of literature are in the library (see *Cutter's* "*Rules*," p. 12). These objects are accomplished partly by the information given in the individual entry and partly by the method of arranging the entries.

Consideration will first be given to the preparation of the individual entries and then to the methods of arrangement. Both processes are necessary for the production of anything that can rightly be called a catalogue. Catalogues are made up of main entries, subsidiary entries (such as series entries and subject entries in a dictionary catalogue), and references. These last are of two kinds: (1) directions from a heading which is not used to a heading that is used, and (2) directions from a heading to another heading where fuller information about a given book is to be found. In printed card catalogues the place of this second form of reference is taken by another copy of the main-entry card with an additional heading written over the first. This is called an "added entry."

A main entry is composed of five parts: (1) the heading, (2) the title, (3) the collation, (4) the imprint, (5) supplementary matter. How many details are given under each of these parts depends on the fullness of the cataloguing, and it is natural that there should be a difference of fullness between the cataloguing of, e.g., rare early printed books and of ephemeral modern fiction. An appropriate standard of fullness should be set up for each catalogue and this should only be departed from for special reasons; e.g. it might be decided to treat English books printed before 1640 rather more fully. For a good illustration of such difference of treatment, see the introduction and frontispiece of the Aberdeen University Library Rules.

CATALOGUING

The heading is the part of the entry which comes first and is chosen for the purpose of alphabetical or other arrangement. Something must be chosen which will distinguish the book best from all other books, in fact the most individual point in relation to it; and it will be found on consideration that the name of the author fulfils this condition best, as it is definite, not liable to change, easily remembered, generally easy to find, and it reduces the book at once to one of a small class, i.e. those written by the particular author. It is preferable to the first word of the title, which is usually vague, unimportant and not easily remembered. Attempts to use the most important word of the title as heading lead to ambiguity and uncertainty.

The heading consists of the surname of the author, followed by the forenames, if ascertainable, rather than the initials, and, if necessary, a qualifying title which is specially required where authors have the same name. The qualifying title may consist of a date (e.g. SMITH (John) 1563–1616), which is very definite, or of a descriptive phrase (e.g. SMITH (John) *Rector of Baldock*), which is generally more useful. It is obvious that there are many classes of publications where no individual authors' names are given (e.g. Parliamentary Papers or Transactions of Societies), and, in fact, the choosing and setting down exactly the right heading for a book is the most difficult part of cataloguing. Rules covering all ordinary cases will be given later.

The title consists of the title of the book as given

on the title-page—not as given on the publishers' wrappers, the cover, the half-title, etc.—together with the names of the editors, translators, etc., and a statement of the edition and the series. In ordinary English practice it is not usual to repeat the name of the author as part of the title, though this is done in the Library of Congress printed cards. The name of the series, if important enough to be given, comes last, within round brackets. Anything added to the title by the cataloguer should be within square brackets, and anything omitted from the title should be indicated by dots ... unless there is a general statement in the preface or elsewhere that the titles are not necessarily given in full.

The collation may contain the following particulars: the format, the size, the number of preliminary pages and of the ordinary pages, the number of volumes, the number of illustrations and their nature. The format is determined by the fold of the original sheet, which is folded once for a folio, twice for a quarto (4to), three times for an octavo (8vo) and three times also for a duodecimo (12mo), but in this case the initial folding is into three instead of into two. Further foldings give the 16mo, 24mo, 32mo, etc. As the size of the original sheet may differ from the Atlas ($36'' \times 26''$) to the Foolscap ($17'' \times 13\frac{1}{2}''$), to call a book an "8vo" does not give much information about its size—to call it a "Fcp. 8vo" would indicate a size of $6\frac{3}{4}'' \times 4\frac{1}{4}''$, but it is not advisable to use these publishers' and paper-makers' terms in cataloguing

CATALOGUING

as there are differences of size even in English papers of the same name, and the terms do not apply to foreign papers. Each folded sheet or section has a "signature," a letter or number which follows in proper sequence in the book, and the way to tell, e.g., an octavo from a duodecimo is to count the number of leaves or pages between successive signatures. There would be 8 leaves or 16 pages in the case of an 8vo, and 12 leaves or 24 pages in the case of a 12mo. In modern books this method often breaks down as machine-made paper yields sheets of any size and there are various methods of imposition for machine printing. (See Williams, *Elements of Book Collecting*, pp. 14–27.)

The size of a book should be given in inches or centimetres, to the half-inch or centimetre—decimal points should not be used. The height of the page (not the binding) should be given, followed by the width when that is more than four-fifths or less than two-thirds of the height. This method gives the shape of the book if it is out of the ordinary.

The last part of a book to be printed is the introductory portion consisting of the half-title, title-page, dedication, preface, etc., and this usually has a pagination of its own in Roman figures. The number of preliminary pages as well as the number of pages should be stated in the entry, except that they are often omitted when the work is in more than one volume. The number of illustrations should not be given unless it is stated on the title-page, and the abbreviation *illus.* should be taken to cover both plates and figures in the text. If there are maps, folding diagrams or tables, the fact should be stated, and a single plate at the beginning should be described as *frontispiece*.

The imprint may include the place of publication and of printing, the name of the publisher and of the printer, and the date of publication. In modern books it is usual to give the place of publication and the date only, the former being often omitted when it is London. Where no date of publication is given in the book itself, it should be added within square brackets where ascertainable. Where not ascertainable then an approximation should be given, as thus [*circa* 1890] or at any rate the century named, e.g. [16*th century*]. It is not informative to the reader to fall back on the statement "no date" [*n.d.*].

The supplementary matter may consist of the table of contents, which is usually only to be set out in composite works by various authors, or to indicate the contents of individual volumes in collected editions; of an annotation which is a short note describing any special points about the book, its authorship, subject, etc.; and of the shelf mark, which is usually given if the books are classified. Annotation is not a necessary part of cataloguing and is too large a subject to be more fully dealt with here.

It has already been said above that the most difficult part of cataloguing is the choice of a right and consistent heading, but the following summary of rules and principles will be found to cover most ordinary cases. If any difficulty is experienced resort should be had to the detailed *Catalogue Rules: Author and Title Entries*, commonly known as the Anglo-American Code, first published in 1908 jointly by the Library Association and the American Library Association.

(1) The heading is to consist of the surname of the author, followed by the forenames, when easily ascertainable, in the language of the author's nationality (e.g. HORATIUS FLACCUS, Quintus), with some qualifying title added where necessary for distinguishing purposes.

(2) In cases of joint authorship, where there are two authors the heading should consist of the name of the first author, followed by the name of the second; where there are more than two, of the name of the first, followed by the words "and others," the full authorship being set out in the title or in the annotation.

(3) Names compounded with a prefix should be entered, if English, under the prefix, if foreign, under the part following the prefix, except in French, where the prefix consists of or contains *Du*, *Des*, *Le*, *La*, *L'*, *Les*,

Other compound names should be entered under the first part.

(4) The forename should be used as heading for ruling sovereigns, popes, saints, and mediæval authors, the English form to be used in cases of doubt.

(5) British noblemen should be entered under the family name, others under the title.

(6) In cases of change of name (including married women) entry should be made under the last name used as an author.

(7) Pseudonymous and anonymous works should be entered under the author's name when ascertainable, otherwise under the pseudonym and the first word of the title not an article respectively.

(8) Publications of societies should be entered under the name of the society; of institutions (e.g. Churches, Universities, Libraries) under the place; of periodicals under their titles; of states, cities and official bodies under their names.

(9) References should be given from the second and subsequent authors in cases of joint-authorship, and, where of sufficient importance, from the names of editors, translators, illustrators, etc.; also from pseudonyms, titles, etc., where not adopted as headings; from striking words in the titles of anonymous works; and, generally, where considered necessary from alternative forms of headings not adopted as such.

(10) References may be given if considered necessary from the first striking word in the titles of works in *belles-lettres* (fiction, poetry, drama, essays, etc.) and, exceptionally, in other cases (e.g. *Eothen*, *Præterita*).

A catalogue composed of entries and references made as described above and arranged in alphabetical order is known as an Author (and title) Catalogue. The alphabetization requires care and presents certain difficulties. The chief principle to follow is that "nothing" comes before "something" (e.g. Brown precedes Browne, New York precedes Newark). Hyphenated words are treated as a single word (e.g. Folk-lore). When the same word is used in different ways as a heading, the order of entries should be as follows: the word as (1) personal name, (2) place name, (3) subject name, and (4) title.

The works of an individual author may be arranged either alphabetically under the titles or chronologically under the dates of the first editions. A common practice is to put the collected works first. Works written in collaboration follow, arranged alphabetically under the second author, the heading with the words *"and others"* coming after, followed by the references in alphabetical order of heading referred to.

It is clear that an author catalogue cannot answer all the questions which may legitimately be put to any efficient catalogue, and to enable it to fulfil all its functions it must be supplemented in some way by subject-headings, and the variety of the catalogue depends on how this is done. There are four main varieties:—

(1) The Author (and title) Catalogue supplemented by a subject-index in which the entries consist of a subject-heading followed by a very short statement of author, title, and date. (Example: the Subject-Index of the London Library Catalogue.)

(2) The Alphabetico-Classed Catalogue, where the entries are given under subject-headings in alphabetical order, supplemented by an author-index. (Example: the subject-lists issued by the Patent Office.)

(3) The Dictionary Catalogue, which consists of a combination of (1) and (2) in one alphabet, omitting the special indexes which are no longer necessary. (Example: the catalogue of the Chelsea Public Library.)

(4) The Classified Catalogue, which consists of entries under subject-headings arranged in logical order, supplemented by author, title- and subject-indexes. (Example: the catalogue of the Glasgow Public Libraries.)

All these varieties of catalogue are complete in themselves and it is impossible to say that one is better than another, though the experienced librarian should be able to say in any given case which is the best under the circumstances. As regards relative size, No. 1 is the least bulky and No. 3 the most bulky.

It will be seen that subject-headings are incorporated in the indexes of Author and of Classified Catalogues, but form the headings of entries in the main list in Alphabetico-Classed and Dictionary Catalogues. In the last case the entries themselves are usually shortened from the main entry under the author (e.g. the author-heading and the title may be abbreviated and the collation and imprint consist solely of the size, a statement as to whether

CATALOGUING

illustrated, and the date), but the portions of the entry are in the same order, following the subject-heading (i.e. author, title, collation, imprint, and annotation, if any).

No hard-and-fast code is possible in the preparation of subject-headings, but certain principles should be observed and applied in each individual case. The first of these is the principle of *Specific Entry*—the heading chosen should cover the exact subject, being neither too general nor too particular (e.g. a book on Cats should be under that heading and not under DOMESTIC ANIMALS. If there is no exact heading to a subject, the next more general heading should be adopted. Scientific terms should not be used except in the catalogue of a scientific library and where there is no generally recognised popular term (e.g. use CAT, not *Felis cattus*, but ASPIDISTRA as there is no popular name for that plant).

The name of a subject is often compound, in which case there should be no inversion of order, unless the qualifying word is distinctly subordinate (e.g. DOMESTIC ECONOMY; but CHEMISTRY—*Organic*). Where there are only a few entries under a heading it is best not to subdivide, as it is quicker to glance through a few entries rather than to master a system of sub-headings. Certain form sub-headings are common to all subjects and should be used uniformly. The most common are *Bibliography, Dictionaries, Essays, etc., History, Periodicals and Societies*, and *Study and Teaching*. Sub-headings under Countries and Cities are more numerous (e.g. *Climate, Geology, Industries, Social Condition*). A uniform list of these should be used, and when it is decided to break up the entries under a heading (e.g. if there are more than ten) *all* the relevant sub-headings should be made use of.

One of the chief difficulties of subject-cataloguing is to decide when local interest becomes more important than subject interest,[1] that is to say, to decide when to enter a book under the place concerned rather than the subject proper. The general principle is that the wider the subject with local interest, the more likely is entry under the place; the more special the subject, the more likely is entry under the subject (e.g. a book on the Geology of Mexico would go under MEXICO; one on the Copper Mines of Mexico would go under COPPER MINES AND MINING). References from the heading not adopted are important. (E.g. in the above example, under MEXICO there should be references to all headings, such as COPPER MINES AND MINING, which contain entries dealing specifically with Mexico, and under GEOLOGY to all headings, such as Mexico, which contain entries dealing specifically with geology.)

All the books dealing with a subject cannot be given under one subject-heading (specific). The more general books, and likewise books on closely related topics, also contain information on the subject, and these should be made available by references. Such references usually run from general to

[1] This problem is also discussed as a matter of classification, see p. 40.

CATALOGUING

particular. It would take too much space to run them also the other way; e.g. refer from DOMESTIC ANIMALS and VETERINARY MEDICINE to CATS, but not *vice versa*. They are an essential part of a dictionary catalogue and the only method by which a conspectus of a whole subject can be obtained in such a catalogue. References should in addition always be given from forms of heading not adopted to forms adopted.

It is quite clear that in the case of general libraries it would be a great waste of effort for each librarian to construct his own tables of subject-headings and references, and in carrying out such work recourse should always be had to some list of standard headings such as *A.L.A. List of Subject-Headings for Use in Dictionary Catalogs*, 3rd edit. 1911, and the *Library of Congress List of Subject-Headings*, which is kept up to date by supplements. The former in the right-hand column of each page gives suggestions for references, while the latter indicates by the use of heavier type where local subdivision is to be used. References should not be added at random, but with a strict eye to the actual book being catalogued.

An Author Catalogue requires completion by the addition of a subject-index, the headings in which are to be compiled on the principles given above. The entries will consist of a subject-heading, the author's name with forenames, etc., abbreviated, brief title, and date; or, if space is of importance, simply of the subject-heading and the author's name, the short title only being given where there are several books by the same author (e.g. there might be an entry FLOWERS. Avebury; Darwin; Henslow, "Floral structures"; Henslow, "Making flowers.")

A Classified Catalogue requires completion by the addition of subject, author, and title indexes, usually combined in one, the references being to the classification numbers and not to the pages. The forms of the entries may be gathered from the following examples:—

Subject entries:
>   RUSSIA, 914.7.
>   RUSSIA. *Soviet Constitution*, 342.47.
>   RUSSIAN POETRY, 491.787.891.71.

Author entries:
>   ROYCE (G. M.), 920.
>   ROYDEN (Agnes Maude), *Downward Paths*, 176.5. *Christianity*, 261; *Women*, 396.

Title entries:
>   *Life's Little Ironies*, by T. Hardy, 823.
>   *Life's Little Pitfalls*, by A. M. Royden, 171.1.

CHAPTER V

REFERENCE LIBRARIES

BY JOHN WARNER, F.L.A.
Chief Librarian, Public Libraries, Newport, Mon.

Reference Libraries differ in size, importance, and in scope. They range from national libraries of the type of the British Museum and the great copyright libraries and departments of great municipal library systems, such as those of Glasgow, Liverpool, Birmingham, etc., down to the small town library; from university, college, and school libraries to private libraries of every description. The majority are general in scope. It is only within recent years that the Special Library, i.e. the library devoted to some specific subject, has come into prominence. Many libraries, general in character, have special departments devoted to particular subjects which are in themselves Special Libraries. Some of our university libraries, and many of the larger American Public Libraries, have been departmentalised, and thus consist of a series of Special Libraries.

The great Copyright Libraries, the State Special Libraries, such as those of the Public Record Office and the various Government Departments, and private Special Libraries, are regarded as the province of the research worker, and, very rightly, admission to these is carefully guarded in order to ensure that accommodation which is essentially for the scholar and the research worker is not occupied by the merely casual reader for whom there is otherwise excellent provision. Theoretically, university, college, and school libraries and the various private libraries are open only to the students and to those for whom they were established, but a very generous interpretation is nearly always placed on their use. Municipal libraries are generally open to all, practically without any formality.

In the largest libraries the clerical work, correspondence, and orders, and even the mechanical work, such as preparing the books for the shelves, is carried out by a special Administration Department. The Administration Department is an important feature of the large state and municipal library systems of this country and the United States. A Cataloguing Department is also to be found in a number of our libraries, but few British Libraries are able to support an elaborate cataloguing section. Where the library is not of a size to maintain Administration, Cataloguing, and other Departments for sectional work, such work has to be divided between the librarian and staff as a whole, and for various reasons the greater part of the work which would normally be performed by these departments is generally allotted to the Reference Library staff.

The late Mr. Walter Powell, of Birmingham, pointed out that too many library systems suffer from the unwritten law which decrees that a municipal library building must consist of reference department, lending department, and newsroom. Every case should be treated on its merits and considered in relation to local circumstances. Many small towns have established reference libraries which they cannot maintain and which could usefully be abandoned in favour of very small collections of useful quick reference books.

Mr. W. W. Bishop, in his *Practical Handbook of Modern Library Cataloguing*, has defined reference work as "The service rendered by a librarian *in aid* of some sort of study. . . . The help given to a reader engaged in research of any sort is what we mean by reference work." Reference work, therefore, presumes the existence of a trained staff. A sound education, personality and address, and tact in the handling of readers, are only a few of the necessary requirements. Mr. J. I. Wyer, in his *Reference Work*, very aptly says that "Reference work exists because it is not possible to organise books so mechanically, so perfectly, as to dispense with personal service in their use." To deal with the legitimate requirements of certain readers is not always easy, and to satisfy them may occupy a good deal of time, and much discussion has been devoted to the amount of time and service which can reasonably be allotted to individual readers. Much may depend on questions which appear to be of quite a trivial nature, however, and librarians in general are very rightly reluctant to inform a reader that sufficient time has been devoted unsuccessfully by the staff to the matter in question. Undoubtedly the principal aim should be to organise the library effectively, and to take every possible opportunity of instructing readers in the use of the catalogue and bibliographical aids. A very useful departure is the "Readers' Assistant" of many American libraries, whose duty it is to assist readers in the choice of books, the compilation of reading lists, etc., and to stimulate that interest between the library and the reader which can be accomplished so effectively by personal contact.

Great Britain contains no outstanding example of reference library architecture in accordance with modern principles,[1] and it is to the United States that we must look for recent examples. After a long period of quiescence a number of notable buildings are in course of erection in this country, but at present they are not very far advanced. Space, light, heating and ventilation, and the prevention of all opportunities for the collection of dust are the first principles for study. Mr. L. Stanley Jast suggests that "A properly designed library is not, or ought not to be, a building containing books, but should consist of books contained in a building. The very moment you enter its doors you should feel the atmosphere of books, and as soon as possible you should see books, and be conscious of books all the time." Dignity, peace, and repose are essential characteristics, especially of the interior, of every reference library building. A site is necessary which

[1] This reproach is about to be removed by the erection of notable reference libraries at Cambridge (University) and Manchester.

REFERENCE LIBRARIES

will suffice for present needs and for future extension. In the case of very large libraries where extensive storage is necessary, a central "stack" is needed. The stack is a framework of adjustable metal shelves rising in superimposed floors one above the other, each generally about 7 feet 6 inches high, and rising in height according to requirements, every other floor being coterminous with the floors of the main building. The floors are generally of some translucent material. A minimum of space only is required for main and minor aisles. The modern tendency is to place it in the centre of the building where artificial light can be used if necessary. This allows the public and staff rooms to be grouped round it in order to gain for them the natural light which is so essential. Mr. Jast contends that in the storage of books the horizontal area is preferable to the vertical area, and in the new building at Manchester, now in course of erection, the stack will be built on this principle occupying one of the ground-floors and running from the back to the front of the building. The two essentials are ease and speed of transference of books from stack to readers, and construction with a view to future extension. Reading and Staff rooms will be designed according to the needs of the library. Access to the stack can be granted to readers only as a special privilege, but practically every library now grants open access to a collection of the works in more general use, including quick reference works and bibliographical aids. These are stored on shelves in the general reading room to which the public have unrestricted access. In the case of the busy reference library it is usual to arrange for special Students' Rooms for research workers. A sound-proof music room is now very favourably regarded in many quarters. Gramophone Rooms have even been suggested as a desirable addition for the modern municipal library, but these are developments on which there is by no means general agreement. Special rooms for special collections are a luxury that can be afforded only by the larger and wealthier libraries. While the stack itself will be constructed of metal, there is a general tendency in favour of wood for shelving purposes in the public rooms on account of its appearance. Separate tables for individual readers are desirable, preferably providing about 6 square feet of table top, with sunk inkwell, a shelf with accommodation for ruler, pen and pencil, a shelf under the table for books and a pull-out slide. Sloping tables for large folios, atlas-cases, book-rests, etc., are also necessary. The floor is best constructed of some silent material.

Ventilation and heating necessitate special attention in districts where the climate is moist and humid, where metal shelves are likely to sweat and where leather bindings, particularly modern leather bindings, are apt to spue. Spue encourages the growth of fungus, and many libraries have found to their cost the need for a careful study of the ventilation problem. In such districts the relative humidity of the atmosphere must be reduced to reasonable proportions. It is too often forgotten that a tempera-

REFERENCE LIBRARIES

ture of 60° Fah. does not necessarily mean that the atmosphere is reasonably dry. Temperature charts should be carefully marked at regular periods during the day.

Generally speaking a reference book is one which is not for the general reader, but is a work of information rather than of recreation. The foundation of every reference library lies in quick reference books—dictionaries, encyclopædias, bibliographies, concordances, atlases, almanacs, catalogues of other libraries, etc. Where there is a lending department attached, all works which are too large or too heavy to be portable, too expensive, or for similar reasons are unsuitable for the lending department, must necessarily find a place on the reference shelves. Highly technical works, long sets of periodicals, publications of learned societies, Government publications, Patents Abridgements, special collections, and fugitive material—newspaper cuttings, prints, lantern slides, illustrations, and loose sheets which can be stored only in the vertical file or in special cabinets—obviously belong to the Reference Library. Extensive collections on specialised subjects, such as law and medicine, are desirable only in very large general collections and Special Libraries. Works of a general nature only on these subjects are desirable for the average library. All books should be collated before they are prepared for the shelves, and great care should be taken in their preparation for the shelves. Fortunately, there is a tendency to reduce the size of the hideous rubber stamps which have defaced so many beautiful books in our libraries, but it is high time that rubber and metal stamps disappeared altogether and their place taken by small embossing stamps. Book plates should be small and artistic.

Apart from books, the reference library has to provide storage for pamphlets, lantern slides, negatives, prints, deeds, plans, maps, gramophone records, motion-picture films, news cuttings, etc., and special storage methods have been devised for all these various materials. Print mounts, pamphlet boxes, the vertical file and deed boxes, etc., are in use in every modern reference library.

Many municipal reference libraries now make definite provision for the loan of books. Such loans are always regarded as privileges and are not extended to quick reference or rare books or manuscripts. The Departmental Committee,[1] while deciding that the question is one to be solved by the experience of the librarian, remarked that: "In general, the larger the library is, the less desirable is it to lend from the reference department, since it is more difficult to anticipate the demands that may be made on it."

For a guide to Special Libraries and special collections we cannot do better than refer to *The Aslib Directory: a Guide to the Sources of Specialised Information in Great Britain and Ireland*, 1928, published by the Association of Special Libraries

[1] The Public Libraries Committee Report on Public Libraries (1927), p. 61.

REFERENCE LIBRARIES

and Information Bureaux. A similar directory for America has been published by the Special Libraries Association, Washington, D.C. In a pamphlet on "The Technical and Scientific Library" of the Manchester Public Libraries, the Special Library is defined as "Special books intensively treated." The intensive treatment includes minute classification, cataloguing, and indexing; open shelves, and special staff. Most of our large cities now possess Commercial Libraries for the use of the business man.[1] Technical and Scientific libraries are also a feature of the public library systems of Birmingham, Manchester, Nottingham, etc. The Science Library at South Kensington is the principal Science Library of the country. In addition there are numerous Special Libraries devoted to specific scientific and technical subjects, controlled by various authorities. Many large commercial and business houses maintain Special Libraries for research work for their own private purposes. Special Libraries devoted to practically every imaginable subject are to be found throughout Great Britain and America, under the control of societies and institutions. Libraries devoted to such subjects as law, medicine, and theology are fairly common. Libraries devoted to legislation and municipal subjects are a familiar feature in the United States, but there are no Special Libraries devoted to Local Government in this country. Practically every general reference library makes at least one special collection, the outstanding

[1] See Chapter XV in this volume.

example of which is the Local Collection devoted to the literature of the locality in which it is situated.

Mr. J. I. Wyer, in his *Reference Work*, already quoted, emphasises that: "The conception of reference work which is limited to the resources of one library or one city or even to books and print alone is out of date. There must more and more be utilised the impressive machinery . . . the effect of which will be to make available in varying degrees, but to every library, the resources of all others." The National Central Library,[1] in addition to the work in connection with its own stock, acts as a clearing-house for inter-library loans between an increasingly large number of general and special libraries, and it is impossible to speak too highly of its work. For University Libraries similar arrangements have been made by the Association of University Teachers' Library Co-operation Committee. Inter-library loans not only in this country but between countries, and photostat or similar methods of reproduction, are proving a boon to thousands of students for whom otherwise certain lines of research work would be impossible. Lectures on various topics and bibliographical demonstrations in the handling and use of reference books, and other forms of extension work, are common to many reference libraries. For such lectures the necessity of obtaining or preparing lantern slides has now been obviated by the Epidiascope, an instrument which allows of the projection direct on to the

[1] See Chapter XIV.

REFERENCE LIBRARIES

lantern sheet of documents, printed matter, photographs, book illustrations, map drawings, typed or written manuscripts, models, etc. With the Epidiascope the objects are, of course, projected in their natural colours.

LIST OF REFERENCES

BISHOP, W. T.: *The Backs of Books and Other Essays in Librarianship.* 1926. Baltimore: Williams & Wilkins. U.S.

McCOMBS, C. F.: *The Reference Department (Manual of Library Economy,* No. 22.) 1929. Chicago, U.S.: American Library Association.

MUDGE, I. G.: *Guide to Reference Books.* Edition 5. 1929. A.L.A.

WARNER, J. *Reference Library Methods.* 1928. Grafton.

WYER, J. I. *Reference Work.* 1930. A.L.A.

CHAPTER VI

LENDING LIBRARIES

BY G. E. ROEBUCK, F.L.A.
Borough Librarian, Public Libraries, Walthamstow

A properly planned, well arranged lending department will be one in which ample floor space, effective natural lighting and ventilation are ensured and artificial illumination and heating so contrived as to be unobtrusive yet effective. It is a department for the short-time use of the public and considerations of personal comfort give place to public convenience. The general atmosphere of the department should be one of well-regulated order and system; a sense of easy and direct access to a large collection of well-kept books. System, and all the "gadgets" connected therewith, should be kept within reasonable limits; not permitted to hinder the impression that one is in a library. Simple precautions should be taken to avoid nuisances arising from congestion at points of service or in the gangways; from overhigh and overlow stacking, and the faulty disposition of literature which causes overcrowding at points avoidable by a more judicious arrangement of the stock. The merits of radiating lay-out for purposes of supervision and the arguments for close adjustment of shelving need not detain us here. The only conditions with which we now concern ourselves are the general appearance

LENDING LIBRARIES

and usefulness of the department, and this can best be summarised in "smartness and efficiency."

Admission to borrowing rights varies all too much throughout the country, but safeguards are usually less persistent in districts where they might be expected to prevail. The old-time hindrances have almost all disappeared. Registration, given essential particulars, should be as easy and prompt as possible. In the early days of the library movement, when indicators were in use and enclosed stacking was the usual thing, defaults less likely to occur were guarded against with rigour, whereas to-day the public access to book stocks has made a bid for public conscience, and only a small minority of library users are found to offend. It is generally ruled that the safeguards necessary in the case of the few are irksome to the orderly majority, and the risk involved in dispensing with them has happily proved to be small.

The registration of borrowers is a most important matter, being usually the first contact with the townspeople. It is essential to remember that the newcomer is probably strange to all about him. Counter staffs are prone to overlook this and press register cards, rules, etc., upon a new customer with an air implying a full understanding on the part of the visitor of all the requirements of the moment and the customs of the establishment. Registration should be dealt with at some place other than the service counter, if possible, because it is difficult to attend properly to a new borrower who stands in a long queue of people anxious to pass the wicket and proceed to the shelves. By assigning a special point for enquiries and registration, where staff trained for these purposes can be stationed, public service is improved and the harrasing effect of hindered counter service is avoided.

The form, size, and material adopted for tickets are largely governed by the method of charging and the staff space available. A ticket which may be sometimes in the keeping of a borrower should be small enough to avoid inconvenience but not so small as to be easily lost or overlooked. For the same reasons it should be of a material likely to stand handling without tear or breakage. If the custom of issuing small and narrow tickets in order to save space in a charging set leads to a less speedy handling, it is poor economy to save space and lose time in service.

Methods of charging vary. Strict "double charging" affords information useful in case of default, but a great number of libraries have abandoned this double check since it is so seldom called into play. Elaborate staff work is all to the good where circumstances permit, but the special employment of persons to undertake such duties may be questioned as largely a waste of effort for little ultimate gain.

The regulations governing use of a lending library should be few and reasonably worded. It is no inducement to enrolment to be faced with a

LENDING LIBRARIES

large sheet of double-columned, small-printed legal excerpts, reiterating pains and penalties for offences which are the least likely intentions of a decent citizen. Lengthy and ultra-legal regulations defeat their own ends—they are either not read or not understood. Furthermore, the extracts from regulations, such as are considered necessary, should govern the use of the book departments; the average borrower seldom visits the newsroom or the children's room, and is unlikely to commit any such offence as sleeping or eating upon the premises. After all, so long as a sound set of regulations govern the institution generally, the less they are forced upon the attention of borrowers the better; at most readers require to know the range and duration of privilege and the means (if such exist) for the extension of either, upon occasion.

The new borrower, equipped with ticket of membership and acquainted with the simple rules governing privilege, requires some introduction to the department. The larger the lending library, the more essential this is. Library workers, accustomed to the surroundings, find it difficult to see a large store of books from the stranger's point of view. Headlines on case tops; flapping or rigid indicating signs to every subject under the sun; "hand" signs pointing on the left to POETRY and on the right to POTTERY—these are real helps when a borrower has found his way about the department, but they stagger the newcomer, especially if they are all docketed wtih mysterious symbols suggestive of mathematical calculation. The ideal introduction would be a personal one, yet few large systems could manage this. A short printed statement with a simple ground-plan of the room is the most busy centres can manage, but this, well done, can be most helpful.

Librarians are so accustomed to catalogues and class lists as to take their usefulness for granted. These need explanation, however, and so does any system of classification.

Assuming that the new borrower does not require fiction, all our "aids"[1] are helpful and bewildering at one and the same time. The person who just wants "a book about Russia," does not know where to begin on a stack of books and is simply aghast at the 150 entries in a typewritten catalogue, despite their most elaborate and helpful annotations. It is here that the Enquiry Desk becomes of real service. Once a borrower has gone through the ordeal of registration and has concluded his first visit to the library, the way to familiarity is clear, but little short of bewilderment results from an unassisted first visit to a large and busy circulating department. This is not the place to discuss in detail the processes by which to overcome the difficulty, but rather to remind library workers that it is a very real one.

The larger number of persons using a lending library are, of course, in quest of lighter reading, and the supply for them should be ample. We have

[1] See Chapter VIII.

LENDING LIBRARIES

yet to rise to the great opportunities of fiction as an educative and cultural agent, and generally let our borrowers loose on rows upon rows of books each, thanks to the monotony of bookbinders' efforts, exactly like its fellows, and we usually conclude that the readers know what they want better than we can tell them. Our only help is an arrangement under authors—or titles—both equally useless if the author or title is not remembered. There is a great good resulting from leaflets,[1] which the public may read at leisure, guiding them to the fiction which has for its *motif* historical, social, political and economic themes—the "purpose novels" as distinct from the purposeless.

The whole subject of guidance, both to the purposes and the location of books, is receiving much attention of late years. The simple handling of this matter is by far the most effective, and the direct guidance to reading in the "bookmark" category often makes a specialised reader, and such a borrower will find extended forms of guidance the more helpful from a simple beginning.

Monotony in appearance of bookshelves is a troublesome concern. All too seldom do we encourage a reasonable variety in this direction. Cut-and-dried prices, under contracts, lead to stereotyped finish; and it is little short of a calamity, to say nothing of an artistic blunder, when a fine large-paper work of authority is bound in nowise differently to a novel of little worth, except in the

[1] Discussed in Chapter XVI.

greater length of the back and additional blind tooling.

The keynote of a modern library should be the "charm of books," yet, alas! many a lending library presents a drab and uninviting appearance through a too casual attention to re-covering work.

Every problem facing librarians in lending libraries to-day arises from the fact that readers, with or without a critical faculty, and often unguided by any definiteness of interest, are passed on to the book stacks. Open Access is too great a boon to need any qualification. So is popular education. Yet even this creates its problems.

Faced with a public that will not make its needs known, the librarian of to-day has to get behind the blank fronts of many of his readers by means of suggestion. This effort may obviously score only now and then. So far as proof goes, it may never succeed, but it is the only course.

With the growth of broadcast influence the critical sense of the public will develop and the librarian must be ready for the extension of public taste. Meanwhile there can be nothing but praise for librarians who contrive by numerous time-taking means to get books of merit and helpfulness into the hands of their readers.

The ideal lending library is, then, an apartment well stocked with the best and most deserving books, easy of access and well cared for. It should be a section to which the local resident is attracted by its smart appearance and one in which he shall not be too bewildered by an excess of directions which are not guidance. It should be a department comprising smart officers in charge of intake and output of books, whose efforts are aided and whose work is simplified by the presence of a capable enquiries and registration officer accustomed to people as well as the books they may require.

Issue is not everything. Time was, in the years during which the library movement was struggling into recognition, when libraries vied with each other in the number of the books circulated, and their value was accounted by the extent of their output. Those days, happily, have gone for ever! Libraries are recognised to-day for what they can mean to the community, and the library system that really serves a hundred townsfolk well may conceivably be doing much better work than one where the circulation touches millions.

CHAPTER VII

LENDING LIBRARY ROUTINE WORK

BY HENRY A. SHARP, F.L.A.
Deputy Chief Librarian, Croydon

Many lending library routine duties are apt to be looked upon as mechanical and even irksome; such things, for example, as shelving, putting into order, and dusting. While this may be to some extent true, they are none the less necessary and valuable pieces of work.

Roughly speaking, the secrets of an efficient lending library lie in tidiness, method, accuracy, punctuality, and unfailing courtesy towards a sometimes trying public.

In the matter of shelving, it should be remembered that "a book misplaced is a book lost"; shelving must therefore be done with care, and all books put into correct order every day. It is usual for a definite section to be allocated to each junior, and he should endeavour to become acquainted with the books in it. Open access causes much wear and tear on the stock, and it is necessary to tidy shelves frequently throughout the day. In some larger libraries, during busy hours, an assistant is kept doing nothing else but tidying shelves and helping readers.

Routine work should be done methodically, and

LENDING LIBRARY ROUTINE WORK

as nearly as possible to a set time-table, remembering that the public service takes precedence over everything else.

Accuracy cannot be too strongly insisted upon in charging and discharging books and in making necessary records. A wrongly discharged book is likely to create bad relations with the public, and a wrongly cast statistical record may involve many hours' work.

With a service going on continuously for many hours, punctuality is essential. No assistant should be allowed to depart until he has been relieved, and it should be a matter of routine for on-coming assistants to be at their posts five minutes before the scheduled time, in order that work may be properly handed over. Off-going assistants should see that counter and shelves are left tidy and clear.

To ensure the efficient carrying-out of routine work some form of staff work-book should be kept, such as a page to a day diary, which is made up each morning by a senior assistant. The hours of duty of each are written at the top, and below is a list of the duties for which each is responsible during that day. Each duty as completed is marked with a double tick (√X), each partly completed one with a single tick(√), and each task not begun with a circle (O). Particulars of special happenings, such as callers, accidents, light failures, etc., are entered as they occur.

Book-dusting should be carried on regularly, a tier or so at a time. Vacuum-cleaners have rendered this work easier and more hygienic, certain types being specially adapted for library purposes. It is not sufficient to draw out the dust from the tops of the books; the shelves require treatment equally, and it is advisable to remove books a shelf at a time.

As all routine work is devised with a view to facilitating the public service, it may be pointed out that nearly all new borrowers, and many old ones, welcome the aid of the staff in their search for books, but are often afraid to seek it, especially during busy times. Wherever possible, an assistant should be delegated to "floor duty" for this work, particularly during rush hours.

Application forms are issued free to residents, whether burgesses or not, and usually to non-resident students and employees. Special forms are often provided for depositors, i.e. non-burgesses who wish to dispense with a guarantee, and for subscribing borrowers, i.e. borrowers who live outside the library district. As the signature of a form presumes cognizance with the rules, a copy of these, or an abstract of them, should be given with every voucher.

When a voucher is handed in, it should be checked carefully to see that the applicant resides in the district, or is entitled to borrow under one of the other provisions, that the necessary full name is given for distinguishing purposes, and that the guarantor's name appears in the accepted record of evidence, usually nowadays an officially recognised local directory.

LENDING LIBRARY ROUTINE WORK

....

Form of Application for Membership of Lending Libraries

——— PUBLIC LIBRARIES

I,..being a ⎰ Ratepayer*
        (Name in full—state if Mrs. or Miss)   ⎱ Resident
                                                                     Student
                                                                     Employee

in the Borough of ...., hereby apply for a Reader's Ticket or Tickets in the class or classes against which I have signed below. I have read the Rules of the Libraries and agree to be bound by them.

    †1. General Ticket (for any kind of book).....................*Signature*

    2. Non-Fiction Ticket ....*Signature*

    3. Music Ticket (for Musical Scores only)....................*Signature*

Home Address..

Business Address or School ....

Age, if under 21..................... *Date*..

      * Cross out the words that do not apply.   Do NOT FOLD THIS CARD
      † Sign for each kind of ticket required.   [See over

FOR A NON-RATEPAYER THIS FORM (IN ADDITION) MUST BE FILLED IN BY A RATEPAYER

I,..being a
        (Name in full—state if Mrs. or Miss)

Ratepayer in the Borough of ...., hereby undertake in default of the above applicant, to replace or pay the value of any book not returned, or which may be damaged by ⎰ him* and to pay any fines or expenses ⎱ her incurred in recovering the same.

Signature..

Address..   *Date*.................

The Ratepayer must be prepared to show evidence that he or she is a Householder or Ratepayer. The production of the last receipt for payment of Rates, or a lease showing the occupancy of a whole premises, or a rent book showing the occupancy of a whole premises, or the appearance of his or her name in a recognised local directory will be accepted as such evidence. The guarantee remains in force until it is withdrawn in writing by the Guarantor.

                  * Cross out the word that does not apply.

STANDARD FORM OF BORROWER'S VOUCHER

A PRIMER OF LIBRARIANSHIP

If all is in order, there is no reason why the applicant should not be allowed to borrow forthwith, in which case the first charge will be made on a dummy ticket bearing his name and address.

```
No. S472.8
Smith, John
21, Limes Rd.
Expires 14 Feb. 1933
```

——————— PUBLIC LIBRARIES

PLEASE DO NOT FOLD THIS CARD

Available at any Lending Library for ANY kind of book.

Notify change of address without delay.

Readers should consult the Card Catalogues, as all books are not shown on the open shelves.

This Ticket is NOT TRANSFERABLE and the person named above is responsible for books borrowed upon it.

BORROWER'S POCKET TICKET

Vouchers are then handed over at set intervals to the assistant responsible for making out tickets.

Borrowers' cards are gradually reducing themselves to a standard form, serving the dual purpose of a ticket and a charging pocket, thereby effecting a saving of time at the issue counter. Distinctive

LENDING LIBRARY ROUTINE WORK

colours are used for general, non-fiction, music, and juvenile tickets. Subscribers' and other non-residents' tickets are similarly differentiated, or alternatively overprinted. The essential particulars are: registration number, name and address, and date of expiry.

If space and staff permit, it is an advantage if new tickets can be claimed at some spot away from the counter, which is at certain times so crowded as to make it impossible for new borrowers to be received in a fitting manner.

The later procedure in registering borrowers is somewhat as follows. The vouchers are indexed by writing the borrowers' names at the head. They are then alphabetised and checked with the borrowers' register, which is formed from the vouchers themselves, to see if any applicant already holds tickets or is a defaulter. They are then numbered serially or by a decimal system, entered into a number book, the numbers carried on to the vouchers, the tickets written and sent to the library to which they belong.

It is economical for all tickets to be made out at one library; in order to know which belong to any library, the vouchers are stamped with a letter before being sent to the registration library, as C for Central. With the vouchers should be a simple form of invoice showing how many vouchers are sent and of what kinds. The registration assistant will add underneath the number of each kind of ticket made out, and a note of any vouchers returned

A PRIMER OF LIBRARIANSHIP

as queries. For statistical purposes, a book giving ticket numbers, and under columns the year of expiry, should be kept; as a ticket is cancelled the number should be ticked off and used up for a new borrower. Renewed tickets may retain the same number. It is thus a comparatively simple matter to calculate the number of tickets in force at a given time.

Registers of guarantors do not seem necessary, but a useful adjunct is a card Roads Register. The name of the road is written at the top, and the rest is printed with numbers from 1 onwards. Every house number having a borrower is marked. This is a useful record in cases of outbreaks of infectious diseases, and especially for carrying-out campaigns for new readers. A glance at such an index will show which roads need to be "whipped up."

BOSTON ROAD [52 houses

1	2	3	4	5	6	7	8	9	10	11	12
13	14	15	16	17	18	19	20	21	22	23	24
25	26	27	28	29	30	31	32	33	34	35	36
37	38	39	40	41	42	43	44	45	46	47	48
49	50	51	52.								

ROAD REGISTER CARD

It is fairly common for a borrower to lose his ticket. On reporting the fact, he should be asked tactfully if careful search has been made for it. If the assistant is satisfied, a Lost Ticket Voucher is

LENDING LIBRARY ROUTINE WORK

issued, for which sometimes a small charge is made as a deterrent, on which application is made for a fresh ticket, which is issued a week or a fortnight later, and is a duplicate of the original, expiring on the same date, but marked to indicate that it is a duplicate. This voucher is filed with the original.

```
..............................          ..............................
           ............ PUBLIC LIBRARIES
           BORROWER'S LOST TICKET VOUCHER
Name in full..................................................................

Residence ....................................................................

Former Residence.............................................................
       (if recently changed)

Date ........................................................................
```

NOTE.—A new ticket will be issued 14 days after the date of this application. If the original ticket is found, it should be returned to the Lending Library to be cancelled.

Borrowers are reminded that they are liable for any books borrowed on lost tickets, even after this application has been made.

LOST TICKET VOUCHER

Card-Charging.—The common form of card-charging is the card-in-pocket system, each book being represented by a manilla book-card, preferably four inches by two, at the head of which is written the accession and class numbers in large plain figures, and short author and title. It is kept in a pocket inside the front board.

To charge a book, the book-card is removed, placed inside the borrower's ticket, and the date on which the book is due to be returned is stamped on the date label.

After the day's statistics have been compiled, the charges are placed in trays on the "return" side of

```
17846        942
Green, J. R.
Short History
        of England
```

MANILLA BOOK-CARD

the counter alongside those for previous days, a date guide is placed in front, and number guides at intervals to facilitate discharge. The arrangement varies. Sometimes it is by accessions numbers throughout, sometimes the non-fiction is placed in

LENDING LIBRARY ROUTINE WORK

front in class order, followed by the fiction in accession order.

```
17846          942
Green, J. R.
Short History
       of England
```

```
No. B861.3
Brown, Ada
17, Long Rd.
Expires 25 Apr. 1931
```

PUBLIC LIBRARIES

PLEASE DO NOT FOLD THIS CARD

Available at any Lending Library for ANY kind of book.

Notify change of address without delay.

Readers should consult the Card Catalogues, as all books are not shown on the open shelves.

This Ticket is NOT TRANSFERABLE and the person named above is responsible for books borrowed upon it.

A "CHARGE"

In charging and discharging books, a simple but useful precaution is to check the accession number on the board label with that on the book-card. If this is done as a matter of routine, wrong discharges are impossible.

Provided a book is not knowingly required by another borrower, it may be renewed for a second fourteen days, and sometimes for a third. In some libraries, fiction, and popular works published within the past year are not renewable.

Renewals may be effected by personal application, by telephone or by post. Some libraries provide printed post-cards for the last method. When a book is brought to the library, it is restamped and a slip placed in the charge with some such words on it as "First Renewal." Where books are not brought, a dummy charge must be inserted at the original date, referring to the date of renewal. Without such a device it is not easy to find the charge when the book is returned, and undesirable disputes may result.

When a book becomes three weeks overdue, a card or circular letter is sent requesting its return. This failing, a second is sent a week later, and if necessary, a third. Borrowers who do not respond to such formal requests are written to politely but firmly, and as a last resource before the matter is placed in the hands of the Town Clerk, the guarantor (if there is one) is applied to. Janitors are often used for making personal application for the return of overdue books.

Nothing is more annoying than to receive a demand for something for which one is not liable. Therefore, before a notice is sent, the charges must

LENDING LIBRARY ROUTINE WORK

be checked with the shelves to make sure that the book in question has not been returned and wrongly discharged.

Fines are levied for the detention of books beyond the specified period, and for damages. The common fine is a penny a week or part thereof.

Damages, which should be assessed by a senior assistant, are usually caused through negligent exposure to the weather, or by domestic animals.

A receipt should be given for every payment made. Cash registers are sometimes used for this purpose, but the cheapest form consists of roll tickets, a roll of a thousand costing tenpence. Books containing numbered tear-off receipts are often employed. For miscellaneous receipts, including damages, replacements, sales, lettings, etc., a counterfoil receipt book should be used.

At the end of each day, or first thing next morning, all moneys received must be checked, agreed with the receipts issued, and recorded neatly in a Receipts Book.

Books other than fiction may be bespoken on payment of a penny or twopence to cover the cost of notification. In some libraries, fiction published more than ten years may be similarly bespoken. The method is for the borrower to fill in a form with the author and title of the book required, and his name and address. The charge is then found in the issue and a bespoken slip inserted. When the book is returned, it is set aside, and the bespeaking borrower is notified; books not claimed within a clear twenty-four hours are recirculated. In cases where for any reason a book cannot be supplied, the borrower should be notified and the fee returned.

Routine duties laid down in connection with books exposed to infection must be punctiliously observed. Opinions differ as to whether such books should be destroyed or disinfected and returned to circulation. The ruling of the local Medical Officer is usually taken, but the second method is the more usual.

On receiving notice from the borrower or the Medical Officer that a house is infected, with library books in it, the charges are immediately removed, placed in a separate tray, and the tickets impounded until the Medical Officer certifies the house as clear. In no circumstances must a borrower be allowed to borrow during the interval, nor must any books be returned direct to the library. Any borrower attempting to do either of these things is severely dealt with under the byelaws. The books are usually collected by the Medical Officer's department, disinfected, and returned to the library. He usually supplies the librarian with a list of infectious diseases and the period for which abstention is necessary. It must be remembered that not only is the patient debarred, but also the entire household.

Borrowers are allowed to make suggestions of books and as to the management of the library generally; the staff should be at all times ready to

LENDING LIBRARY ROUTINE WORK

encourage this privilege by drawing attention to the book provided for the purpose.

Besides statistics of stock, the essential statistics peculiar to a lending library are of:

>Issues
>Cash Receipts
>Inter-library loans and discharges.

Records of daily issues are first made at intervals during the day on a rough issue sheet ruled for non-fiction classes and fiction. When the day's issue has been counted up, the results are carried into an Issue Book. In some libraries there is a very detailed form ruled into 80 columns. This not only tells the number of books issued, but provides information as to the *kinds* of books read. It affords invaluable information for the librarian in his scheme of book selection.

300	320–330	340–360	370	380	390	400	500	510	520	530	540	etc.

PORTION OF DETAILED ISSUE BOOK

A Receipts Book shows what moneys have been taken, and is arranged in some classified form, as: fines, damages, bespoken books, replacements of lost books, sales of publications, and lettings.

Statistics of borrowers are dealt with briefly earlier in the chapter.

Those relating to inter-library loans and discharges presume the availability of tickets at any library within the system, and will show how many books have been lent from one library to another, and how many borrowed from one library and returned to another.

It is necessary that stock of a lending library be taken at intervals. To facilitate this, a shelf register is provided, which is a record of the books as they should stand on the shelves. It comprises the stock number, author and title, and is usually in the form of quarto sheets ruled in columns. The procedure is for one assistant to call over the books on the shelves and their stock numbers, in case there may be duplicate copies, and for another to mark with a tick in the appropriate column. The issue, binding, withdrawal, and reserve records are afterwards treated similarly; books not then marked off are searched for, and if necessary recorded as "missing." The custom of closing for annual stock-taking is dying out, and it is becoming more general to take stock of a few classes each year, while the library is still open.

Although accession methods are not peculiar to lending libraries, a few remarks on them are admissible here on the ground that the greater number of books pass into them.

The sources of a library's book stock are mainly: purchases on the librarian's recommendation after

LENDING LIBRARY ROUTINE WORK

approval by the Libraries' Committee; readers' approved suggestions; gifts.

Dealing with the first, it should be a rigid rule that all books purchased are obtained upon an official order, setting out author and title, publisher, edition (where necessary), and price. One copy of the order should go to the vendor, the duplicate should be retained for checking purposes. The order form should indicate that, unless otherwise stated, the latest edition of a book is required. If the order is a long one, such as a Book-List, copies of that list may be attached to the order. The suggestions slips which have led up to the purchase should be stamped with the date of order and filed behind the vendor's name guide.

Upon receipt, the invoice, suggestion slip and actual book should be carefully compared to make certain that the book is as ordered. The date of receipt is stamped under the ordered date on the slip, which is then placed behind the title-page. Where several copies of a book are purchased, the slip goes into the copy which is the one to be used for cataloguing purposes, usually the Central one.

The books should be entered forthwith into the Accessions Book and the number carried into the book itself. This accession number, or the block of numbers concerned, may then be carried on to the invoice. By this means it is reasonably certain to ensure that every book added passes into the library, especially if the back of the title-page is at the same time defaced with a process-stamp, similar to the following:—

Lib.	No.
Class X	X
V.	P.
Cut	Cata.
Sta.	Ann.
Pl.	Subj. I.
Bk. C.	Check
Acc. Bk.	
Sh. Reg.	Apprd.

PROCESS STAMP

A study of this stamp will show that the processes involved before a book is ready for circulation include: cutting, stamping, plating or labelling, book-carding, accessioning, shelf-registering, cataloguing, annotating, indexing of new subjects, checking of these three last processes, and a final check.

The necessity and importance of all these processes speak for themselves, and the reasons for them are obvious.

CHAPTER VIII

AIDS TO READERS

BY R. D. HILTON SMITH, F.L.A.
Deputy Librarian, Hendon Public Libraries

Aids to readers connotes all the measures designed to promote the full and understanding use of libraries by their patrons. Such fundamental aids as catalogues, guides and indexes to the classification, and the humane planning of departments are dealt with so fully elsewhere[1] that it is proposed to cover here a few characteristic developments in other directions.

There is no more important aspect of library work than personal service. Its chief elements are, of course, the personality, knowledge, and resource of the staff; but these qualities can usually be systematised to yield the best results with the utmost economy of effort. In the successful treatment of any enquiry there are certain principles which can only be assimilated, unless the young assistant is given special direction, through long practical experience and a process of trial and error. The librarian's best means of securing the maximum use of the capacities of the staff in comprehensive personal service is for him to compile, in the light

[1] *See* Brown and Sayers, *Manual of Library Economy*, 3rd ed., 1931; Sayers, *Manual of Classification*; Stewart and others, *Open Access Libraries*, 1915, and other chapters in this Primer.

of local circumstances, an exhaustive manual covering the essential points. The following analysis of one only of the enquiries with which an assistant may be confronted from day to day is offered as an illustration:

Upon enquiry for a specific subject take the reader to the shelves and show him what is available. When there is a fair representation of books, leave him to make a final choice and avoid forcing special books upon him. If there is nothing in, take him to the catalogue, show what is stocked, and explain that any book may be reserved. In a case of urgency, try to obtain a suitable book or books from some other library in the system. If this is unsuccessful refer the matter to a senior officer or the librarian. Failing success here finally offer to obtain a book from or through the National Central Library.

Notes.—1. The subject may be represented in another Department of the library or in a general work not shelved with the subject.

2. Record all enquiries in which difficulty is experienced in the Register of Enquiries.

3. Never send a reader away unsatisfied without the clear understanding that he will enquire again within a specified time or await notification from the library.

4. Even if you believe the reader to be perfectly satisfied, always ask as he leaves whether he has found what he wanted.

AIDS TO READERS

Instructions like these, covering every conceivable species of enquiry and every method of tendering unobtrusive assistance, not only give a sound grasp of the principles and technique of personal service, but save much labour or possible omissions in the training of newcomers.

A valuable extension of personal service can be effected by following up the expressed preferences of readers. For example, if a reader in the course of a bookish conversation with a member of the staff stresses a particular preference in reading or any difficulty in tracing all the literature of his favourite subjects, here is an opportunity for the preparation and despatch of a special reading-list. Whether the list shall be suggested first is a matter for discretion, but for obvious reasons it is usually better to send it without previous mention. In experimenting on these lines over only a short period it has been found that quite unsolicited lists on various subjects have been gladly received and well used by the readers. The discovery that his preferences or antipathies are remembered engenders in the reader a warm regard for the library and its activities. For this reason, every assistant should develop to the fullest possible extent an associative memory for names or faces and literary tastes.

Allied to the direct personal assistance of readers is the question of systematically recording and keeping in close touch with enquiries which cannot be met forthwith, so that no single request, however casual, is overlooked. This can be secured by means of a register of enquiries. All the machinery necessary is a ledger or thick exercise-book and a set of small tickets of stout pasteboard, say an inch square, numbered serially from one to one thousand or beyond. The ledger has columns for: Serial number of enquiry, Date, Author, Title or Subject, Resources tried by library, Decision, Final Result, Date. Upon an enquiry for a book not in the library or books on subjects which seem to be inadequately represented or not represented at all, the assistant concerned enters details in the register, marks the entry with a serial number, gives the enquirer the corresponding number-ticket, and asks him to hand in the ticket in a week's time, when the book required, or further news of it, will be available. Weekly, or more often, the register is examined and it is decided whether a book shall be bought immediately, held over for the next book-purchase list, borrowed from the National Central Library or some other source, or whether no action shall be taken. The decision is briefly entered in the relevant column and steps at once taken to put it into effect. When the book is received, or if it cannot be obtained at all or some delay is inevitable, this is noted in the Final Result column as "Awaiting borrower," "o.p. and unobtainable," "Trying other Libraries," and so on. On the return of the reader with his ticket, either the book itself or exact information concerning the action taken for his enquiry is therefore available. The system has many advantages. Firstly, an

AIDS TO READERS

assistant can make an entry with great ease and rapidity because of the elimination of all but essential detail: this is an insurance against a casual enquiry being overlooked under pressure of other work, particularly counter work. Secondly, the reader holds, instead of the recollection of an unsuccessful enquiry, a tangible record that his needs are receiving attention. Thirdly, a periodical review of the register reveals weaknesses in the stock, the adequacy or otherwise of the liaison with other sources of supply, and the real manner in which the library is meeting the, at any rate articulate, demands made upon it.

Measures such as these provide adequately for the definite, expressed requirements of readers. But the vast majority of readers have no articulate desires, or their desires are vague. They linger and they browse and they are, for the most part, open to guidance and suggestion.

Next to personal recommendation—perhaps in advance of it—the most powerful suggestive agent is the attractive display of books. Passing with bare mention the question of exhibitions, Christmas and holiday literature displays, and the extremely valuable use of the book-jacket as a kind of ambassador for its parent book, let us concentrate on small displays in the lending library.

Probably the best way of showing small collections to the greatest advantage is by means of troughs for ten or a dozen books. The base should be at a good angle so as to tilt the books backward and show the titles clearly, and the back high enough to prevent the bigger books from obscuring the title-label at the top. If the whole back from base to top is cork-covered, differently sized labels can be affixed without trouble as occasion requires. The troughs can be accommodated—of course, where circumstances permit—on tables, the tops of low book-cases, special narrow ledges affixed to any available wall, sometimes at the counter. Where space is particularly scarce, occasional small shelves can be arranged at the ends of island bookstacks or across pilasters or columns.

The advantages of special displays are these: they assist the reader who does not know what he wants until he sees it; they attract the attention of the interested reader to books of whose existence he may be unaware; by bringing together for the time being books on cognate subjects which are ordinarily separated on the shelves, they reveal new aspects of the subject; they afford the shy enquirer that dumb assistance which will help him most; and, through the enormous power of suggestion acting on the minds of those who are receptive to a fresh atmosphere, they entice to new adventures in reading. From the domestic standpoint, they help the librarian to dispose of that undesirable phenomenon the unused book. In every library there is an amazing number of books which remain unused, through the merest accident of position on the shelves, title, binding, size, or some other extraneous cause. Without special "pushing" these books tend to become part of the furniture; but if judiciously and gradually introduced to readers amongst attractive displays they have a better chance of active survival.

The subjects for display are legion, and by degrees the whole library stock can be isolated in small groups at one time or another. But the success and public appreciation of displays hinges largely upon the devisal of good *titles*. Excellent and even popular books in a display bearing an ordinary title remain unused, but a captivating title helps to circulate even the most unlikely books. The simple experiment of showing the same books under different headings proves this in a remarkable way. Compare for example, the bald heading *Some books on the Supernatural* with the richer and more appealing *Dreams, Ghosts, Witchcraft, and Magic : books on the inexplicable and uncanny*, or *Domestic Economy : selected books* with *The Home : selected books on furnishing, cookery, decoration and minor repairs*. The chief principle in securing an attractive title is to give an enticing twist to a familiar subject, but several other interesting forms of title can be devised. For example, the use of a brief and telling quotation—*"The Glory of the Conquered" : books on the great failures of history*; a simple question— *What do You Know about Words?*; an injunction— *Learn a Language : some useful books for beginners*; a dictum from an eminent man—*"The Ten Greatest Novels of the World are Russian"—Arnold Bennett*; the simple use of an adjective—*Ten Attractive Autobiographies* or *Some Notable Books on Education*.

Suggestions for new titles can be found in the inventiveness and ingenuity of the staff, dictionaries of quotations, general reading and newspapers, the titles of books, the adaptation of ideas derived from almost any source.

Finally, there is a display which can be made the most serviceable of all, through its value as a personal link, *The Staff have read these books and recommend them*, or, less positive and therefore less effective, *Books recommended by the Staff*. In even a small library the reading of the staff is usually sufficiently wide for a catholic and interesting selection of a dozen books always to be available. Other displays should be changed at least monthly, but this can safely be made permanent. Readers develop in a very short time a remarkable faith in the suggestions of the staff and it is doubtful whether there is any form of book-suggestion which can equal in value, appreciation, and popularity a carefully arranged display of this kind.

Reading lists do not differ greatly in function from book-displays, although they are probably less effective. Precisely the same principles as to subject and title apply, and a good list can form a similar enticement to books, bring related subjects together, and help in the exploitation of the unused book. But whereas the constantly changing titles on displays are a sufficient indication of their periodical replacement by others, some more active means of advertising new reading lists is necessary if they are to receive due attention. This can be

AIDS TO READERS

effected by continual variations in size, colour, paper, format, and phraseology of titles; but it is an excellent idea to keep always to the same style of printing, so that all publications in that style eventually become identifiable at once with the library. The use of a dignified slogan, invariably printed under the name of the library on all lists, is a similar notion, and there is no better slogan than Cleveland's *Books—Information—Service*.

In the compilation and lay-out of short reading lists, cataloguing practice should be eschewed, for the catalogue and the reading list are entirely different things, based on different principles and performing distinct functions. The list should be rigidly selective, attractively annotated, and so arranged that the more valuable books appear, regardless of alphabetical order if necessary, on the optical centre, i.e. the top third of the page. Pleasant variations in appearance can be effected by occasionally printing title before author or omitting author's initials and using spaces instead of punctuation for the division of the entry.

For a discussion of various kinds of lists and reading courses and more detailed treatment of all the subjects covered by this chapter the student is referred to the writer's "Aids to Public Library Readers" in the *Library Association Record* for December 1930, pp. 263–274.

CHAPTER IX

CHILDREN'S LIBRARY WORK

BY W. C. BERWICK SAYERS, F.L.A.
Chief Librarian, Public Libraries, Croydon

Libraries now attempt a service for children which parallels in a degree that of the adult library. In older libraries an alcove or a few shelves in the adult library were nearly always provided; and so long ago as the fifties Manchester had rooms exclusively for children. In the eighties there was a special library for them at Nottingham, and in the nineties the reading-halls at Cardiff, which were combined reading-rooms and reference libraries, were established for them by Sir John Ballinger. In a few favoured towns there were excellent libraries for children, and among them may be named Chelsea, Hampstead, Islington, and Stepney.

Want of means prevented greater development, but the principle was recognised, for in 1917 the Library Association declared that "library work with children ought to be the basis of all other library work." Naturally, then, with the removal by the Libraries Act of 1919 of the penny rate limitation, a gradual growth began in the number of children's libraries. That growth continues. The resulting libraries differ in quality according to means and in kind according to intention. The county library has recognised children from the beginning, and, indeed, lends books very largely to them as well as to adults. In the towns it is accepted that every public library must now have a special room, which is named according to local predilection the Children's Library, the Junior Library, the Young People's Room or the Juvenile Department.[1]

This room should be a good one, if possible, but it is more important to supply books to children than that they should wait for handsome accommodation. Work can be begun even in very small rooms. Whenever practicable, however, they should be well ventilated, warm, and have good natural and artificial light, especially when they are used as reading-rooms. They should be readily accessible, and it would be better if they were not approached by stairs. Some librarians think they should have separate entrances from the street, but this is not essential.

The decoration of the room should be simple, but attractive and unofficial, plenty of colour being introduced. Bare wall spaces should carry good pictures, which need not necessarily be pictures for children, and I recommend the introduction of flowers and ferns. The windows should be curtained; blinds are also desirable for use when there are lectures during daylight.

There are various methods of arranging such a

---

[1] This ugly name has fortunately become rare. With it, we hope, will go the horrid booksellers' jargon of "juveniles" as meaning books for children.

library which differ because of the intention of the librarian. The complete children's library unites within itself all the activities of an adult library; that is to say, part of its shelves carry a lending library and another part books for use in the room only, and in this room there are periodicals. The furniture can sometimes be folded so that the room can be used for lectures or other meetings. There may be a second room for story hours and reference library purposes in some of these libraries. The most complete example of a library of this description is the Boys' and Girls' House at Toronto, where a whole building is devoted solely to children.

Another system is that which is seen at Westminster and elsewhere. Here the department consists of two rooms or one room divided by a high glass screen into two parts. One of these is a lending library, the other is a separate reading-room.

A third system, which has been worked out with considerable thoroughness at Manchester, is a reading-room only. Here the children come to the room to read the books in it under the supervision of the librarian.

The arguments for these three systems may be summarised:—

The complete library provides everything the child needs, and trains him from the outset to an understanding of all the purposes and possibilities of a public library.

The second system, where division occurs, is based on the assumption that the movement occa-

CHILDREN'S LIBRARY WORK

sioned by the choosing of books for home reading will disturb children reading at the tables, and discipline will be difficult.

The reading-room system is based on the belief that reading in itself may or may not be good, but reading pursued by children limited in number to those whom the librarian can know personally will ultimately produce the best results. In the last case the children get their books for home reading, as at Cardiff, from an elaborate system of school libraries, or from the adult lending libraries, as at Manchester.

The successful children's library has free access to shelves. The shelves should not exceed 5 feet in height, or be more than 3 feet in length. Tables and chairs should be lower by about $1\frac{1}{2}$ inches than those used for adults, and there should also be some very small chairs and quite low tables for tiny children.[1]

Display stands for picture books are, like all other library furniture, made by library supply firms. In allotting wall space one wall could be left dull white or, better still, be silvered, to serve as a lantern screen. There should be baize screens to carry separate illustrations and notices. It is usual to have a counter with exit and entrance wickets.

[1] There is sometimes a doubtful regulation which limits the children's department to children from nine years of age. This rule must exclude a great many children, especially girls who, in working-class districts, are very often "mothers" of their tiny brothers and sisters. There is no difficulty in admitting little children if a proper children's librarian manages the library.

A PRIMER OF LIBRARIANSHIP

The wickets have a value in controlling large groups of children, but they are not always necessary.

The selection of books is an extremely difficult work. The great classics for children, of which *Pilgrim's Progress, Robinson Crusoe, Alice in Wonderland, The Water Babies* and the *Jungle Books* may serve as examples of the score or more of such books that exist, should be the basis of the library. These should be bought to saturation-point, and in the best editions available. Books must be, for physical and aesthetic reasons, on good paper and have good, legible type, and be well bound. About 60 per cent. of the library may be fiction, but non-fiction need not consist of definitely children's books only, but should include books ostensibly for adults which children will read in travel, the sciences, the useful arts, history, and biography. New books should never be added until they have been examined. Bowdlerized and re-written editions of classics and works written in crude dialects or baby slang should be avoided, as well as ill-printed or badly illustrated works.

In America children's libraries open from about 9 a.m. to 6 p.m., apparently during school hours. In England the library should not be open in school hours but during the lunch recess (12.15 to 1.45 p.m.) and after school until bedtime (say, 4.15 to 7.30 p.m.). On Saturdays and holidays the hours may approximate to those in America (say, 10–1 and 2.30–5.30). Children are admitted on

CHILDREN'S LIBRARY WORK

the recommendation of their teacher, who is thus brought into contract with the library in an official capacity. It is usual to allow the child under twelve to have one book at a time, but older children sometimes have the privileges of adults.

The rules for the management of the library should be the fewest and simplest: requiring cleanliness, discipline in the room, care of the books, prescribing for their reading at home, and providing against the possibility of infection through books. Parents and children should understand that damage to books must be paid for, and fines not exceeding one penny per week are sometimes, but not always, imposed for overdue books. The librarian, however, should have complete discretion in remitting fines for sufficient reason. He (or more probably she) should be empowered to suspend the membership of ungovernable children.

The activities of the library are many, but the main purpose of them all is to create a more intelligent use of literary material. In most libraries there is an activity called a Story Hour, which has for its purpose the opening of important books to children who would otherwise pass them by. Stories are told to groups of about thirty children, although much greater groups are sometimes served, and should be graded to suit the age of the children. In this, and in lecture work for children, voluntary aid is often sought by librarians, although one or two libraries employ a story-teller as part of the staff. Lectures, which may be illustrated, are usually simple and on general subjects; rarely are courses offered. These activities are so popular that admission is usually regulated by a simple form of ticket, on the back of which lists of books are sometimes printed. In some libraries lectures are given alternatively to boys and girls. Usually, however, the sexes are mixed, but may wisely be divided during the lecture.

Classes of children are brought to some libraries during school hours by their teachers, and undertake the reading of some subjects chosen by the teacher under his direction. The librarian is given notice of the visit and collects the necessary books from all departments of the library. Other classes come to be taught by the librarian in the arrangement of the libraries, the use of catalogues, the proper handling and the care of books, and the use of reference tools. This lesson is particularly valuable for children about to leave school, but is often given much earlier. Other activities we have met in libraries have been children's reading circles, stamp clubs, dramatic societies, musical classes and rambling clubs.

One very popular activity is the collecting of illustrations from old books, magazines, catalogues, and other sources, which are cut out and mounted by the children as a pastime. These, mounted on uniform sheets and classified, form a valuable encyclopædia of illustrative material which is useful for illustrating special subjects and events. Teachers may draw upon it for class work at school. Some

CHILDREN'S LIBRARY WORK

libraries have collections approximating 60,000 such illustrations.

A few libraries now issue a special children's library magazine. At Croydon a *Junior Library News*, consisting of an imitation typewritten magazine of four pages, has appeared for eight years, and is being continued in printed form. Leeds and Hendon are two other libraries which have such magazines. Their contents consist of notes, announcements, short reading lists and lists of new books.

Contact with schools is maintained in some towns by means of school libraries, which are collections of books deposited in each school and changed at intervals, very much upon the lines adopted more recently in county libraries. The largest system of this kind is at Cardiff, and is controlled by the city librarian. Where these libraries do not exist and the children borrow from the public library itself, the children's librarians endeavour to visit each school, public and private, in their area once during each term. This enables them to compare notes with teachers, to distribute library literature, occasionally to address classes of children, and in various ways to make the libraries auxiliary to the official education system.

The whole success of modern children's library work depends upon the children's librarian. A distinct and specialised training exists for children's librarians in America, and in England the need for it is extending and is being gradually recognised.

A PRIMER OF LIBRARIANSHIP

So far, however, children's librarians have received the ordinary library training plus experience in particular libraries where children's work is in vogue. There is a short course every second year at the University of London School of Librarianship. The initial education of the teacher, especially the kindergarten teacher, makes a sound basis for this work, but ordinary library training should be added, with a special intention towards children. Candidates for this work should be lovers of children, but without sentiment, should have good health, be good disciplinarians, and have faith in the work.

In the limited space I have been able to devote to this subject it has been impossible to exhaust it. There is literature on various branches of the subject, and under the guidance of the Editor of this work I am writing a much more detailed manual to be entitled *A Manual of Children's Library Work*, which will be published shortly.

CHAPTER X

COMMITTEE WORK AND OFFICE ROUTINE

BY CHARLES NOWELL, F.L.A.
City Librarian, Coventry

Public library committee work differs materially from that of any other department of municipal activity, owing to the legislation governing public libraries, and, in particular, to the clauses concerning the delegation of powers[1] and rate limitation,[2] which latter, from 1850 to 1919, crippled the library movement in a way that no other local activity has had to experience.

Any library authority has been able to delegate the whole of its library powers to a committee specially appointed for the purpose. This committee can be (in Scotland must be) augmented by a number of non-council members selected for their expert knowledge in one or other of the subjects represented on the shelves of a library. Libraries have been, therefore, generally administered by committees which did not report to their local councils except annually. They were only allowed to spend the limited amount—at the best the proceeds of a penny rate[3]—and, moreover, it was a

[1] 1892 Act, Section 15, Sub-section 3.
[2] 1892 Act, Section 2, Sub-section 1. For Scotland and Ireland the rate limitation was extended to 3d. in the £ in 1920.
[3] Except, of course, those towns which had promoted local acts to increase the rate limit.

committee composed in part of members who were not directly responsible to the electors.

In many cases this resulted in the local authority taking little or no interest in the development of the library system, but under an enthusiastic committee many a librarian was able to worry through the critical period and develop a library service so efficient that some local authorities obtained private legislation authorising an increased rate to be levied for library purposes.

To-day we have a confusion in committee methods which is the direct result of this early legislation. By the abolition of the rate restriction in 1919 (so far as England is concerned), the work of the library committee can be placed in exactly the same relationship to the local authority as that of the other committees, which, with the exception of those under partial government control (such as police and schools), are governed by the same regulations throughout. Generally, however, we may say that although all other committees report and recommend at regular intervals to the local authority, library committees, because of this former practice under a restricted rate, operate variously all over the country. In many cases the delegation of powers has been continued—sometimes, unfortunately, with the absurd "rate in the pound" bogey still persisting. In other towns the change in legislation was rightly interpreted as bringing the libraries into line with other departments. The complete delegation of powers was withdrawn, and the library committee

COMMITTEE WORK AND OFFICE ROUTINE

made subject to the same rights and restrictions as other committees.

At this point it will be worth while, I think, to outline an efficient system of committee control, showing how the work of the local Council can be expedited without this responsible body losing control of the essentials of local government.

Although committees report monthly (or—but more rarely—at longer intervals) to the local councils, this is not to say that the committees have no delegated powers. Some local authorities, for example, request their committees to submit their minutes in three sections. The first section includes what are known as "special recommendations," special reports, items which involve serious additional expenditure, those which constitute an important departure from present practice, or resolutions which need, legally, the confirmation of the local authority. The purchase of land for a branch library, the raising of loans, and alterations in bye-laws are examples of items which would appear as "special recommendations."

The second section—"minutes for confirmation"—deals with variations in policy and practice which are not sufficiently serious to be classed as "special recommendations." This section, in short, contains the remaining resolutions of the committee which are not covered by the delegated powers. "Minutes for confirmation" would include such items as additions to staff, the abolition of newsrooms, or the inauguration of a school library service. It will be seen that the first and second sections differ only in degree, but they both differ essentially from the third section in that the minutes can be debated, and approved, postponed, or referred back. They can be rejected, even, though that course is seldom taken.

The third section—usually the largest—includes the minutes which the Council cannot debate, amend, or alter in any way. Questions, however, can be asked. No other action is permitted, for these minutes are all concerned with detailed administration, the powers for which have been delegated to the committee. The Town Clerk, as Clerk to the Committee, decides the appropriate section for each resolution.

Standing orders covering these arrangements might read as follows:—

(a) Matters which committees submit for the special decision or for the special information of the Council shall be submitted in the form of reports or of recommendations; and the matters to be so submitted shall include those for which the committee possess delegated authority, but which involve, or appear likely to involve, a new departure in policy, or expenditure substantially in excess of that contemplated by the Council at the time authority was delegated to the committees; and in case of doubt whether a delegated matter ought, under this Standing Order, to be submitted as a report or recommendation, the Mayor shall have power to decide the point, and his decision shall be final. In regard to delegated matter submitted as a report or recommendation, the committee concerned shall take no action pending the consideration of the report or recommendation by the Council.

COMMITTEE WORK AND OFFICE ROUTINE

(*b*) The Town Clerk shall arrange the reports, minutes, and recommendations of committees in such order as may appear most convenient to the Council. The reports, minutes, and recommendations of each particular committee shall be considered in immediate sequence, and the recommendations of each committee shall be considered before its minutes.

(*c*) The minutes of each committee, as distinct from its recommendations, shall be divided into two sections: (1) minutes which need the confirmation of the Council; and (2) minutes which do not need that confirmation as being within the statutory or delegated powers of the committee.

With these powers the public library committee can budget for their requirements in exactly the same way as other committees; there should be no question of "levying a rate," but of estimating expenditure. These estimates—in common with other departmental estimates—are then considered by the Finance Committee (probably the most powerful committee of any local authority), and the original estimate and the report of the Finance Committee concerning it are then considered together by the Council. Thereafter, for all ordinary routine and normal administration the committee are in complete control of the library, with financial control to the limit defined in the accepted estimates.

Some librarians and members of committees may object to this supervision by the Council, more particularly, perhaps, in view of the publicity usually given to Council proceedings in the local press. They fear the results of any adverse criticism made, and that important proposals might be rejected. My only comment on this would be that the duly elected representatives of the ratepayers have the right to such a control, and committees must be prepared for criticism by having a good case submitted by capable representatives. The increased publicity, in the case of an efficient library service, is helpful; the control, nominal. Where the library is weak and inefficient it can hardly be adversely affected by any change in control.

This development in library administration in many places has led to an increased allotment from the rates which would have appeared incredible to the librarian of twenty years ago. And it is not only in this way that the library service benefits. By becoming a Standing Committee of the Council the Chairman, Vice-Chairman and officers have an improved status, and the membership of the committee is held in respect—where formerly there was little or no competition for Council vacancies.

The regular discussion of library matters in the Council meetings does not militate against the efficiency of the library service, for it is found that the general body of councillors take a keener interest in the work of the libraries, and the old idea of giving the libraries a round sum each year, and requiring (at most) only an annual report on work accomplished, is rapidly giving place to a more sympathetic consideration to the needs of the department. In this change the librarian himself plays an important part. By his tact, ability, and close association with the Council and chief officials he can enlist

COMMITTEE WORK AND OFFICE ROUTINE

their interest and sympathy with results entirely beneficial to his department.

Although many librarians still act as clerks to their committees, there is an increasing tendency to make the Town Clerk the official responsible for the minutes of all committees. Naturally, he works in close co-operation with the chief officer of each department. He will prepare and distribute the agenda, but the librarian will send him most of the items to be included. The Town Clerk will be responsible also for the attendance book showing the record of attendances of each member. Similarly with regard to accounts. Formerly librarians were entirely responsible for all book-keeping. Now it is more general to have the book-keeping centralised in the Treasurer's office, and he must keep the library accounts in such a way as to give the librarian the information he desires. The Engineer, too, is made responsible for all buildings, including the libraries. These arrangements do not restrict unduly the freedom of activity of the chief officer. The librarian still approves the minutes in draft, he is still responsible for the checking of all accounts, and he also advises the Engineer as to structural defects to be remedied, or alterations and repairs to be effected.

In all too many cases the work of the library committee is largely a matter of routine, and varies little from month to month. This is unfortunate, for it will tend inevitably to a slackening of interest on the part of the members.

A PRIMER OF LIBRARIANSHIP

The book service is the most important service offered by the library, and yet there are some who say that the committee should leave book selection entirely to the librarian. Although the librarian is (or should be) thoroughly equipped to advise on all sections of book service, the committee should have control of the main stream of new books added. One method (and one that is to be commended) is to give the librarian the following powers:—

(a) To buy second-hand books at his discretion;
(b) To purchase for class revision to definite amounts (sanctioned, if considered necessary, by the committee);
(c) To purchase important new books between committee meetings, subject (where considered necessary) to approval by the chairman.

This gives a freedom of action which, with a competent librarian, will be of inestimable value to the public library he serves. I may add, however, that in very large libraries the librarian has wider powers, and only books considered at all doubtful would be submitted for approval.

Books so submitted, if approved, should be ordered as soon as possible, although if second-hand or review copies are possible within a reasonable time, a circular list of "Books Wanted" can be sent to selected booksellers with advantage.

The most satisfactory method for book orders that I know is an order form in triplicate. The first copy is retained by the library, the second and third are sent to the bookseller—the second copy is re-

COMMITTEE WORK AND OFFICE ROUTINE

tained by him, and the third used as a delivery note and returned to the library with the books. This delivery note is subsequently attached to the corresponding invoice before the accounts are sent to the committee for approval. Explanatory notes are, of course, clearly printed on each copy of the book order.

Care should be taken to see that the committee are kept informed of the general library activities. Nothing irritates a man more in his public work than to learn from the newspaper, or some other unofficial source, of new developments by the committee of which he is a member. The committee should receive advance copies of every publication issued by the library, and gifts should be officially reported to and accepted by the committee before any other action is taken. The monthly report should give full information regarding the progress of the various institutions under their control (avoiding details of administration wherever possible), dealing with staff, departmental activities, issues for the previous month, gifts offered, and any special recommendations from the librarian. Important recommendations frequently involve a longer report, which should be given an individual number on the agenda. Reports concerning the staff are governed, generally, by Standing Orders of the Council, for most local authorities now have a special committee to deal with staff and salaries, and each departmental committee must be kept informed of many details which were formerly settled by the chief officer himself. The record of issues should be shown by departments and by classes, with the corresponding figures for the previous year, and only accurate figures should be included. Judging from statistics published by some libraries, this proviso is to be emphasised.

Sub-committees can be appointed to consider and report upon the details of any library activity, as may be determined from time to time by the committee. Generally, the committee can delegate its own powers to any sub-committee of its own members. The small library is probably best served by having all questions brought before the full committee, with one exception—the accounts sub-committee. In his own interests the librarian should see that the committee have this opportunity of examining all accounts submitted for payment, though usually this is a Council instruction to all committees. The larger the library service the more necessary are sub-committees for books, staff, buildings, branches and extension, lectures, etc.

The procedure for calling the sub-committee is exactly the same as that for the library committee, and if the sub-committee have no delegated powers, the minutes are subject to confirmation at the next meeting of the full committee.

In describing the office organisation of a public library I have of necessity to distinguish between the needs of the small library and those of the larger library systems. In the public library with no branches the librarian has the control of the library

COMMITTEE WORK AND OFFICE ROUTINE

at his finger-tips, and all correspondence will naturally pass through his hands. However small the library may be, an efficient office routine is most desirable.

All correspondence should be dealt with, where possible, by the librarian himself. In this way he will keep in close touch with every phase of library activity. This is not to say that he never delegates any of the work entailed, for in the majority of the medium and larger libraries this division of labour is a necessity.

In medium and large libraries the post every morning will be examined by the clerk, who despatches such items as periodicals, returned overdue notices, reserve cards, and other routine items to their respective departments. Some librarians prefer to open the rest of the correspondence; others allow their clerks to open all except personal letters. The letters, etc., are then roughly classified in order of subject and importance, anything urgent being placed first.

The librarian then clears as much of the correspondence as possible, immediately on his arrival, by dictating to his clerk. The letters needing reports from departmental librarians are pigeon-holed and these are collected within the next hour. Letters circulated to one or more members of the staff for information or action should be covered by a small slip showing the process of circulation, and the work to be done:—

Circulated to:

Deputy Librarian ....

Chief Assistant ....

Chief Cataloguer ....

Branch Librarians: North Branch ....

South Branch...... East Branch...... West Branch......

This letter to circulate to those ticked, and to be returned to the office as soon as possible.

Note.—A star indicates that the individual concerned is responsible for dealing with this letter.

Date..........................

Much of the correspondence in a library is of temporary interest, but some of value, not only as a library record, but as contributing to the information service of the library. It is customary, therefore, to have two correspondence files, one permanent, one temporary. The temporary file is in alphabetical order of correspondent, and is usually removed from the vertical files to transfer cases at the end of twelve months. It is wise to preserve this file in annual sequences, and destroy after about five years.

The permanent file should be arranged by subjects, and these in two main divisions—administration and service. The administration section is, of course, limited to buildings, staff, equipment, fittings, extension work, lectures, and the ordinary routine of library work.

The service section includes all that correspondence giving book information to borrowers which

COMMITTEE WORK AND OFFICE ROUTINE

may be required again, such as reading lists, information concerning local history, etc. In the larger libraries each departmental head will preserve this file in his own department, he having been responsible in the first place for the information given. It is in effect a correspondence "Information file." It is best kept separate from the Information File proper, for it is primarily private correspondence, and the actual letters should never be handed to other borrowers seeking the same information, the relevant portions being copied, rather, for that purpose.

The first section should be classified—preferably using a recognised scheme of classification which has stood the test of time, such as Jast's "Classification of Library Economy, Administration, and Office Papers." For the "service" correspondence use the book classification.

For ordinary purposes these subject files suffice, although some librarians prefer to have in addition a name index, which records all the correspondence they have had with each firm or individual. This name index gives briefly the date of the letter and its classification number.

Carbon copies should be kept of all letters sent, and filed with the incoming letter. In many cases copies are made on the back of the letter to be answered. This saves a certain amount of work in the filing, prevents the loss of the copy, and, of course, saves paper. Press copies are not necessary except where legal proof is required.

A PRIMER OF LIBRARIANSHIP

Every library system, however small, should have a typewriter and, if possible, a duplicating machine, which in the small library can be made to serve all sorts of useful purposes—notices, booklists, circulars, etc.

CHAPTER XI

UNIVERSITY LIBRARIES

BY R. OFFOR, B.A., PH.D., F.L.A.
Librarian of the University Library, Leeds

University Library administration is not capable of the standardisation that is to be found in municipal libraries. Abroad, universities are often State-controlled institutions which conform to a type, and their libraries are organised on uniform lines. Books from one French university library are lent to another university library merely as the result of a ministerial decree, but in England the inter-loaning of books is a purely voluntary arrangement with a relatively limited scope. In Prussia a Gesamtkatalog of the State Library and of the twelve university libraries is now being prepared for press: it is difficult to conceive of such an enterprise in Great Britain.

A description of university librarianship in this country cannot, then, be based on universality of procedure. We must divide the libraries into certain groups. Oxford, Cambridge, and Dublin have copyright privilege, and so are semi-national libraries. It may seem strange to put on one side the greatest university libraries in the country, but their problems are largely those appertaining only to national collections. The Bodleian and the Cambridge University Library, too, are more detached from the work of teaching than is the case of a single college or "unitary" university; and the University of London Library at South Kensington is in the same position in this respect. The Scottish University libraries are all ancient foundations with traditions of their own. They once had copyright privilege. Aberdeen is still a semi-national library for the north of Scotland.

Scottish libraries may, however, be included with the modern university and university college libraries of Great Britain and Ireland in a more or less homogeneous group, at least thirty in number, although even the modern universities differ widely from each other in their library organisation. Thus the description given here is subject to severe limitation in its scope, and even so must be based largely upon individual experience.

The library is usually regarded as a distinctively academic department, the Senate or corresponding body reviewing the recommendations of the Library Committee, the members of which are mostly its nominees. In Scotland the Court nominates half the number nominated by the Senate; in England the Council in some instances has certain representatives upon the Library Committee. This practice affords an opportunity of enlisting the sympathies of a benevolent and interested layman, but as a rule the active members of the Committee are the representatives of the teaching staff, for it is from the professors and lecturers that almost all the initiative comes in such matters as the purchase of books.

UNIVERSITY LIBRARIES

The Chairman of the Library Committee is usually a professor, for it is he who must carry the business before the Senate. Even if the librarian is on the Senate it is well for him to have the backing of a prominent member of the professorial staff.

The composition of the Library Committee depends to some extent upon its functions. If a good deal of spending power is entrusted to it, then it is a small body that can meet fairly often to consider requests for the purchase of books. But if, after the sessional allocation has been made, the initiative in this respect is entrusted to faculty sub-committees, or to the head of the department concerned in conjunction with the librarian, then meetings of the main committee need be infrequent—once a term, or only at the beginning and end of a session. Such being the case, there is no reason for considering as unwieldy a Library Committee which has representatives from every important department: it is on the same footing, and should have the same dignity, as the board of a faculty.

The librarian is usually the secretary of the committee. It is only natural that nowadays he is seldom not a full graduate. In some cases his academic record has almost exclusive weight, preliminary library training being a secondary consideration. Such a course is by no means an unqualified evil for the good standing of the library; *willy-nilly* it is an attitude academic bodies will always be liable to take. The danger is that the librarian may not have his heart in administrative details as much as he should have. In other cases library training may take first place with laudable results, but a bureaucratic librarian may be so immersed in rules and regulations as to be out of touch with his academic colleagues. A balance has to be struck between academic and administrative qualifications, a thing not always easy to do.

The University Grants Committee has repeatedly recommended that the librarian be a member of the Senate with professorial status and remuneration. Certain institutions have given effect to this (with most satisfactory results), but not the majority. It is probable that the character of the librarian has been a prominent factor, and it has not always been possible to regard librarianship as if it were on all fours with the professorship of a teaching subject. Occasionally the librarian is on boards of faculties, and in some universities he gives courses of lectures which must be restricted in number if he is to carry out his duties efficiently. In this way he is in active touch with staff and students.

The assistant library staff is recruited in such various ways that it is difficult to lay down hard-and-fast rules. There is often a senior grade composed mainly of graduates, with a sub-librarian as second in command. The persons in such a grade have the title of "assistant librarian": they undertake cataloguing and classification, answering bibliographical questions, and so forth. There is another grade of "library assistants," not by any means composed of persons of inferior capacity in their own

UNIVERSITY LIBRARIES

line, who attend to business details, such as ordering and entering books, correspondence, and the like; many librarians can testify to the excellent service they render. As libraries grow, the first class tends to become larger at the expense of the second. Its members are often selected from a library training-school, but local graduates have a powerful claim. Thirdly, assistants may be appointed who are afforded the necessary facilities to attend such lectures as will give them a degree if spread over a longer period of time than that taken by the ordinary student. One university library that has done this has given their present librarians to three prominent university libraries. Some universities also encourage their assistants to take the examinations for the Library Association diploma.

At one time all suggestions for purchases were scrutinised by the Library Committee, but this method became too tedious. By allotting a certain sum to each department the initiative in the purchase of books passes to the head of such a department. The librarian may ask for reconsideration when he thinks fit, but if a professor has made up his mind that a certain book should be bought from the amount allocated to his subject it is difficult for anyone to say him nay. Faculty sub-committees may, however, exercise direct control in examining the lists of books suggested for purchase: this more particularly applies to the medical library, which is often separately organised.

Each university has its own method of financial

allocation. The amounts vary considerably, but by no stereotyped method, according to the size of the department. Unspent balances should not be allowed to be carried forward indefinitely, but should, at the end of each session, be pooled for the benefit of the general library fund. The great difference between a university library and a municipal library is that the former has to set aside a very considerable portion of its funds for the purchase of periodicals and works in continuation—a figure often amounting, if the cost of binding such volumes is included, to 50 per cent. of the total grant. Another difference lies in the great number of books of foreign origin that the university has to purchase. A certain sum is earmarked for general purposes. The more generous this amount is the better, and if the librarian is worth his job its control will be left to him. Apart from books of a general character there are special collections to be kept up which may not be peculiarly connected with any one subject.

It is best for the librarian to have the detailed accounts kept in his own department by the usual double-entry methods. Bills are initialled for payment by the accountant after the periodical meetings of the Finance Committee. Sometimes the librarian himself is permitted to draw cheques up to a certain amount, but it seems desirable that all payments, other than petty cash items, should be made by the appropriate administrative department—that of the accountant.

It has been pointed out that professorial sug-

UNIVERSITY LIBRARIES

gestions give the most important impetus to purchase. Suggestion-books are the rule, but they are cumbrous and unnecessary if forms are employed and properly filed. Much the better method appears to be that evolved by the University Librarian of Manchester, where 5 in. by 3 in. cards are used; buff for new books, blue for second-hand works. Headings are assigned for all the appropriate details—title, author, publisher, price, lot number, and in a parallel column accessions number, fund, and actual cost. These cards can be filed simply as to whether the books have or have not come. In some cases order or suggestion forms are retained as accession slips, with the addition of the appropriate details, slips also being made for the whole volume of each periodical and for donations. Thus is formed a complete record for census purposes, but it is somewhat unwieldy; an accessions book seems handier with its progressive numbers, the latter being also put on the back of the title-page and upon the catalogue slips.

Entries of periodicals are often made in ponderous ledgers, but cards are much simpler. A card of fair size, divided up into a number of squares, has a longer life than a single line in a ledger: in each square is inscribed the number of part and date of arrival, a blank square keeps vividly before the eye the non-arrival of a particular part, and a metal clip can be fixed to the card as a warning. The cards can be labelled or coloured according to the interval of publication—yearly, quarterly, monthly, and so on;

thus each representative group can be checked at the correct periods by means of a general index.

The author catalogue is the chief, often the sole, catalogue, and is compiled very fully. Subject catalogues are unusual and where they exist are not greatly used. The library staff is so small that all its energies are required to cope with the author catalogue: the teaching staff naturally impart bibliographical information in their respective subjects, and an enormous mass of material is embodied in sets of periodicals and thus escapes classification.

There is no uniformity in classification. Some adopt the Library of Congress system, still more employ Dewey, but perhaps as many more have either fixed press marks or expanding methods of their own, the academic curriculum not agreeing well with Dewey's decimal symbols. In consequence, one method is simply to stamp each book with the name of the subject, and within this limit to classify according to the broad divisions, putting the books into alphabetical order in each division. Elaborate classification, long groups of symbols and segregation into groups of ten by draconic methods, are not popular with the university reader.

Access is one of the major differences between a university and a municipal reference library. The latter is usually "closed," and books cannot be taken from the shelves by a reader. The great majority of university libraries, on the other hand, admit some kind of open access. The stock at Newcastle is thrown open to the staff, "research," and honours students. At Manchester certain subjects are allotted to particular rooms and admission is obtained by application to a member of the library staff. At University College, London, and to some extent at Leeds, recommended students are given keys, a system carried very far at the first place, where many hundreds of keys are in circulation. None of these expedients have found universal favour. It seems probable that in the future the liberality of Cambridge will be a general model, and every member of the university will then have the privilege of browsing at will along the shelves, at any rate for all the books that are likely to be in any demand.

Valuable books and special collections will require greater security. It is security that most university librarians pine for more than anything else. In future accessibility must go hand in hand with security: a generous policy in the former involves effective supervision of the exit from the library, a thing not always understood in university circles.

Departmental libraries constitute the most difficult problem which a university librarian has to face, but it is impossible to deal adequately with it here. It is a less serious matter for the older universities where the library is of great dimensions and can complacently shed some of its branches. But with the newer ones it is different: in some instances practically the whole of the science books are housed in the various departments, and even many of the arts departments have developed "class" or "seminar" libraries which rival in magnitude the corresponding section in the main library. Thus the central collection may be left with the flotsam and jetsam of half the subjects in the curriculum.

The one great reason for this practice is the need for quick reference when the university buildings are scattered over a wide area. Fortunately, this tendency finds as small favour in many academic circles as it does with the librarian. The lines between all subjects are more blurred than was once thought to be the case, and a reader may not always know which particular building will contain the book he wants. "General honours" as well as "pass" degrees, and "subsidiary subjects" spread the readers' field over a wide area. Moreover, departmental libraries are notoriously ill-controlled; the librarian has not his eye on them, and so lacks interest in their upkeep: the books are either too accessible and gradually disappear, or they are so locked up that few but the professor can get at them. In the new circular building at Leeds the library will occupy so central a position that the chief science departments will be at no undue distance from the books they want, and there will be an outer ring of alcoves on two floors, each of which may be shut off as a room if so required.

Smallness of staff makes a sufficiently comprehensive register of borrowers a great problem. There should be three registers—one of borrowers, another of the books borrowed, and a third of dates when the

UNIVERSITY LIBRARIES

books are due back. The clerical work thus entailed is tedious, and if readers could generally be induced to do this work[1] by means of carbon copies an enormous amount of time would be saved.

The lending of books from one library to another is governed by a scheme described by Colonel Newcombe in his article on Regional Libraries and the National Central Library.[2]

Finally, university libraries occupy a rather detached position in the British library world, and if the University and Research section of the Library Association can succeed in remedying this undesirable position it will be all to the good.

---

[1] This course is now followed in some university libraries, including that of the University of London. [2] *See* Chapter XIV, page 154.

CHAPTER XII

LIBRARY EXTENSION WORK

BY LIONEL R. McCOLVIN, F.L.A.
Chief Librarian of the Public Libraries, Ipswich

Many—indeed most—public libraries to-day are engaged in various activities, additional to the normal basic work of providing and circulating books and information. These activities, which are embraced under the rather vague heading of "library extension work," are intended to serve one or more of the following purposes:—

(*a*) To interest readers in fresh aspects of literature and life;

(*b*) To create new readers and attract more people to the library; and

(*c*) To associate the library with intellectual and artistic activity, making the library to some extent a centre for the cultural life of the community.

How far a library can wisely engage in extension work must depend upon circumstances. The more essentially "library" functions of the institution must have first consideration. Nevertheless, it is now generally agreed that such activities form a desirable and legitimate part of our work and are a valuable means of improving the use of the library by the public, and increasing its influences.

Lectures are the most usual extension activities, both with children and adults. Series of popular

LIBRARY EXTENSION WORK

lectures, illustrated whenever possible with lantern slides, on a variety of unrelated subjects, are generally preferred, since though it may be objected that they are of limited educational value, they undoubtedly appeal to a wider public, often interesting those who are not yet readers, and initiate and stimulate a desire to read non-fiction. Definite courses of lectures on a special topic, such as are organised by University Extension Committees, while they are more advanced and more limited in their appeal, are, in a different way, of great value. The best plan is to arrange the two types concurrently.

All manner of themes—excepting the party-political, or religious, or controversial matters which are treated in a partisan spirit—are suitable. Literary subjects are naturally most appropriate, but history, biography, science, travel, art, and sociology will figure in a well-balanced scheme. Travel is undoubtedly the most attractive to the general public, perhaps because it lends itself to lantern-lecture treatment. Local history, topography, and literary and other associations deserve special attention, while lectures on the book—its history, manufacture, illustrations, and on the use of reference works, such as dictionaries and encyclopædias—are an invaluable aid to readers.

Musical Lectures are also of considerable appeal; they should, of course, be backed by a good music collection. With the aid of a gramophone they can be well illustrated. Some libraries make a special feature of these gramophone lectures; a few libraries have held them regularly at frequent, even weekly, intervals and maintained good audiences. Local music dealers will generally be glad to co-operate by lending gramophones and records.

Interest in the drama can be furthered by Dramatic Readings of classical and good modern plays. Companies of staff and friends can easily be recruited. To get the best results readings must be carefully prepared and rehearsed, the parts suitably cast and—even though there will be no "acting," costumes, or properties—the players should make entrances and exits, stand, sit and move as in a performance; the old-fashioned method of having all the characters always seated on the stage, *a la* Christy Minstrel troupe, is fatal to good results. It must be remembered that for all copyright plays permission to perform must be obtained and generally a small fee paid. The fact that it is a "reading" and that the public are admitted free of charge does not in any way remove the need to make proper arrangements regarding performing rights. The same, it may be said, applies to the gramophone, or other, performance of copyright music.

Readings of poetry and other non-dramatic literature are often given. Local talent may be encouraged by devoting evenings to the poetry, the compositions, the plays, etc., of residents and natives.

Wireless Listening Groups are often organised to meet at the library regularly to listen to the various educational courses broadcast by the B.B.C. The

LIBRARY EXTENSION WORK

listening-in period is then followed by discussion, preferably under the direction of a leader who has knowledge of the particular subject.

All lectures, etc., should be related to the books in the library, select reading-lists being circulated among the audience, the lecturers being asked when possible to refer to books on their subjects, collections of books being displayed in the lecture-hall and issued to those present as extra, "privilege," issues, etc.

Lectures should, naturally, be held on the library premises, unless this is impossible, as thus they serve to bring people to the library and are associated more closely with the library work. A great many libraries have a special lecture-room. Accommodation for between two hundred and three hundred is a fair average, too small maybe for popular events but not too large for more specialised lectures attracting but a score or two. A good lantern, screen, reading-desk, and platform are essential fittings. In planning the lecture-room provide a second entrance at the platform end, and make the platform as large as possible for dramatic events.

A few libraries have cinematograph projecting apparatus; if ordinary films are used this must be in a separate fireproof room—but there are many non-flam films available, so this is not essential. Projectors—such as those of Evans Brothers, or the Epidiascope—which enable actual objects and illustrations in books, etc., to be shown on a screen are very useful and economical, saving the cost of making slides. The projector will, however, supplement and not supersede the ordinary lantern-slide and lantern. A wide range of slides can be hired, but it is a good thing for the library to gather together its own collection of slides of local and other frequently used illustrations.

The legal position of lecture work is a peculiar one. Unless the town has power under a local Act, it is not strictly permissible to expend money on lectures and the like. Neither is it legal to charge for admission. Some auditors, however, will not object to reasonable expenditure; or it may be defrayed by collections, or out of special funds.

Lecture Work with Children is probably even more valuable than that with adults. Practically the same range of subjects is available; lantern illustration is more desirable. If arranged in co-operation with the schools, lectures will be an excellent means of attracting new children to the library. Use each lecture as an opportunity to tell the children about the library and how to join it.

Story-hours—or, better, half-hours—are a popular and excellent feature of work with children, folk- and fairy-tales, stories from history, extracts from literature, etc., being read or, better, *told*, to fairly small groups of young people.

Exhibitions—again not necessarily always of a purely literary or bibliographical character—can serve the same purposes as lectures. They can range from elaborate exhibitions staged, for periods of weeks, in the lecture-room, to the display, in show-

LIBRARY EXTENSION WORK

cases in the entrance-hall or a room of the library of a few books or objects of interest. Unless there is a separate Art Gallery Committee responsible for this work—and perhaps even then by mutual arrangement—exhibitions of pictures and prints should be organised from time to time.

Holiday Exhibitions—of current literature regarding railway, holiday resort, shipping, and tourist facilities, supplemented by guide books, works on travel and local history, maps, time-tables, etc., are much appreciated during the spring and summer months. Often suitable lectures and exhibitions of slides are arranged in association with them, when much help can be obtained from railway, shipping, and tourist companies.

The work of local educational, artistic, literary, scientific, and other *societies* should, as before said, be linked up with that of the library. These societies may be granted the use of the lecture-room for their lectures and meetings, perhaps freely, perhaps on payment of necessary expenses for lighting, cleaning, etc., but care must be taken to ensure that such receipts do not bring the Library into rating.

Under the heading of "extension work" one may also include the rather different question of providing a service for those who cannot take advantage of the ordinary library provisions. For example, there are the *Blind* who require books in Braille or Moon type. It is a library's duty to ensure the supply and distribution of literature for the blind—unless this is being done adequately by such an organisation as the local Blind Society. In any case, there should be co-operation. A small basic stock should be supplemented by regular borrowing from that great institution, the National Library for the Blind, to which the public library is more than justified in subscribing amply from its funds.

Similarly, public libraries have a duty towards those in hospitals, homes, and institutions, to which books should, when possible, be lent. In the case of medical and surgical hospitals it will generally be impossible to lend and exchange books, but small collections might well be deposited there permanently, the staff assisting in the selection and maintenance of the hospital library. With mental hospitals, however, periodically changed loan collections are quite practicable and are particularly valuable. Almshouses and workhouses also welcome the loan of small collections of suitable literature.

Another similar extension service in seaport towns is that of lending books, through such organisations as the Seafarers' Education Service, for the use of seamen.

In brief, the ideal behind this type of extension work is that the circumstances of readers shall not be a bar to the proper enjoyment of literature; indeed, where the reader cannot take advantage of ordinary facilities the librarian's responsibility is greater than otherwise.

CHAPTER XIII

COUNTY LIBRARIES

BY MISS A. S. COOKE, A.L.A.
Librarian of the Kent County Library

In this short survey of County Library work only a bare outline can be given of details of administration, general organisation, and of the special problems with which a County Librarian has to deal. The history of the County Library movement has been dealt with in the books by Mr. Duncan Gray and Mr. R. D. Macleod,[1] which also give full details of schemes as they were organised ten years ago.

The preparation of books for circulation is on the whole similar to that of a municipal library. For a rural county the selection of books needs to be of a fairly elementary nature and an ample stock of duplicates of more popular books is necessary. It should be remembered that if 250 centres are being served, and the books exchanged three times a year, it takes at least eighty years for a single copy to reach all centres. As many as twenty-five copies of popular books may therefore be necessary.

Cataloguing is simplified considerably as the Headquarters Library is not open to the public,

---

[1] Duncan Gray: *County Library Systems, 1922.* Grafton. R. D. Macleod: *County Rural Libraries, Their Policy and Organisation, 1923.* Grafton.

and the catalogue is only a working one for the use of the staff. Nor is there any need for elaborate shelf guiding, as the staff only have access to the shelves.

The chief point of difference in the preparation of books is the necessity for a double record of the issue of a book. There must first be some card or ticket by which to record the issue of a book from the Headquarters Library to a centre, and, secondly, one to record the issue of a book from a local centre to a borrower.

Different methods are in use in various counties, but the following is recommended, as it allows for expansion without reorganisation and is quicker and less laborious for the Headquarters staff and for the local librarians.

Every borrower is given a fiction ticket and one or more non-fiction tickets. These tickets are supplied from Headquarters, but are made out and given to the borrower by the local librarian.

Each book has two tickets and one catalogue card. When a book is issued to a centre, one ticket is kept at Headquarters arranged in alphabetical order of author behind the name of the centre to which the book is sent, the second ticket—a coloured one to avoid confusion—is left in the book until that book is issued by the local librarian to a borrower. The ticket is then taken out and put in the pocket of the borrower's ticket. These tickets bear the accession number of the book, its author, title, and classification number, and are filed by the local librarian behind the date on which the book is

COUNTY LIBRARIES

issued—or by the date when it is due back, whichever is preferred—and the tickets are arranged in numerical order of accession number. The catalogue cards are kept by the local librarian as a record of all books which are at the centre and may also be consulted by the borrowers. This method entails no writing on the part of the local librarian and no typewriting of lists by the Headquarters staff.

Whereas in a municipal library service the people come to the Library for their books, a county library service must take books to the people. Centres of distribution must be established at every focus of population, and it is one of the first duties of the county librarian to become thoroughly conversant with the whole area to be served and to plan a scheme whereby, if possible, no reader is more than two miles from a centre.

When a centre is to be started, it is usually advisable to call a general meeting at which the county librarian explains the nature of the scheme and the facilities which it offers. A local committee should be elected and a suitable person appointed to act as honorary local librarian. The committee should also arrange hours of opening and other details of local administration.

The choice of place in which to keep the books needs careful consideration. It must be centrally situated, and places which have a definite religious or political bias or which are the headquarters of any one organisation should be avoided, as the centre must be open to everyone. Where there is a

Village Hall an attempt should be made to secure this as the library centre. The Elementary Schools are not wholly satisfactory as centres, because they are apt to give the people the idea that the library is only a school library or that all the books are of an educational nature.

In most counties there are certain places which are too large to be adequately served by an ordinary village centre and which need a service more akin to that of the municipal library, with a building used only for library purposes, a paid staff, possibly a reading-room, and a small collection of ready-reference books. The practice, now fairly general, is to establish these branches on what is known as a differential rating basis.

The books are provided from the Headquarters library and the cost met by the general county library rate, but any other expenses incurred, e.g. rent, salaries, provision of newspapers, shelving, lighting, cleaning, etc., are charged as a special rate levied by the County Council on the town concerned.

The provision of county library branches is fully dealt with in the County Libraries Report, 1929-30, published by the Library Association, to which readers are referred for further information.

Transport

There are three methods of transport in use:—

(1) *Circulation of books in boxes.*

Collections for the various centres are made up

COUNTY LIBRARIES

at Headquarters and the boxes despatched by rail or carrier. Notice of their despatch is sent to the local librarian, who is responsible for calling in all books in the previous collection, checking them, and returning them to Headquarters. It is usual to make an exchange of books at every centre three or four times a year. The number of books sent varies according to the size of the village and to the use made of the books.

(2) *Delivery Van.*

In some counties the collections are made up at Headquarters but taken to the centre by the library's own van, the previous collection being checked and brought back on the same journey. This saves considerable delay and also enables the county librarian to visit the centres and discuss any matters with the local librarians.

(3) *Exhibition Van.*

The third method is to have a van in which the books can be arranged on shelves and to which the borrowers themselves can come and choose the books. The county librarian or an assistant travels with the van—but should *not* drive it—and so is able to meet the local librarians and the readers, and if necessary give advice on the choice of books, etc. For rural counties this method of transport is most strongly recommended. The people much prefer it, as they feel that they have a very definite part in the library, and to country people the sight of a van full of books is a real joy. Many articles have been written on this aspect of the work, and there is no space here to describe in detail the work at a centre.

One of the most important of the county librarian's duties—and one of the most difficult—is to make the library and all its facilities widely known. Country people are surprisingly conservative and it takes a long time to convince them that every type of book is available and may be borrowed without charge.

The county librarian should be ready to give talks on the library and about the books which are available, and no opportunity should be lost in bringing the library to the notice of the people. Articles should also be sent frequently to the local newspapers.

Books, catalogues, leaflets, etc., can usefully be displayed at all Agricultural Shows, Women's Institute Exhibitions, etc.

Catalogues, Handlists, etc.

Users of the county library are not usually able to come to the Headquarters Library to consult a catalogue—they may live thirty or forty miles away from the county town. Some form of printed catalogue is therefore essential. Probably the best and most economical method is to issue a series of handlists on various subjects which can be brought up to date from time to time. County readers are slow to ask for books and shy of confessing that they do

COUNTY LIBRARIES

not know the names and authors of books on the subject in which they are interested. Lists of books, with annotations if possible, make it easier for them, and may perhaps encourage them to explore new fields of reading.

Everything should be made as easy as possible for borrowers to obtain special books. Local librarians are provided with forms on which readers can write the name of the book required. These forms are forwarded to the Headquarters library, and the request is dealt with as soon as possible. It is a mistake to hold back the book until the next collection of books is sent to the village. Many county libraries now organise a special postal service to students. Books are sent direct to the reader, who may have three books—other than fiction—and may keep them for one month.

Co-operation with the National Central Library[1] and with other libraries in the area enables the County Library to obtain for students practically any book needed.

The County Library is a definite part of the programme of the Education Committee and the county librarian is therefore able to keep in touch with all adult educational activities. Books should be supplied from the County Library to all adult evening classes, Workers' Educational Association groups, University Extension Lectures, etc., and the students informed that they may borrow other books to continue their studies.

[1] *See* Chapter XIV.

A PRIMER OF LIBRARIANSHIP

The County Library movement is still in its infancy. The scope of these libraries is likely to extend very greatly within the next ten years. The county librarian must therefore organise the scheme on lines that allow for ample development, the book stock must be built up on sound principles and the library must be kept untrammelled by narrow rules and regulations.

CHAPTER XIV

LIBRARY CO-OPERATION AND THE NATIONAL CENTRAL LIBRARY

BY LUXMOORE NEWCOMBE, F.L.A.
Principal Executive Officer and Librarian, National Central Library

Every student of librarianship must know something about the great movements for co-operation between libraries which have developed so rapidly since—and largely as a result of—the publication of the Report of the Departmental Committee on Public Libraries in 1927. As it is possible in the short space available to give only a brief outline of the subject, an endeavour is made to refer students to sources from which further information may be obtained.

The main recommendations of the Departmental Committee are based on two possible developments in the library service of the country. The first of these is that libraries should be grouped in a series of regional areas, and the second is that at the back of these regional areas there should be a central library, assisted by a grant from the National Exchequer, and having the status of a national institution.

The function of a Regional Area may best be illustrated by details of the first fully organised Regional System: that covering the counties of

Cumberland, Durham, Northumberland and Westmorland. With one or two exceptions, each library in the four counties has agreed to place its non-fiction books at the disposal of any other co-operating library. These libraries include the four county libraries, nearly all the urban libraries, the university libraries at Durham and Newcastle-upon-Tyne, and most of the special, or institutional, libraries. A Regional Library Bureau has been established in the Library of the Literary and Philosophical Society at Newcastle-upon-Tyne. The function of the Regional Bureau is threefold. First, it houses and keeps up to date a union catalogue of the non-fiction books in all the libraries in the area: secondly, it receives and deals with all enquiries for or about books from any co-operating library; thirdly, it acts as a link between the local library and the National Central Library. The Northern Regional Bureau commenced work on January 1, 1931. A special staff has been appointed to compile the union catalogue, the Carnegie Trustees having made a grant of £3,000 for this purpose. It is estimated that the work of compilation will take three years. When the union catalogue has been compiled it will be kept up to date by each library supplying an entry for each non-fiction book added to, or withdrawn from, the library. The Bureau staff—probably one full-time, or even part-time, assistant—will incorporate this information in the union catalogue, and will deal with the forms of application received each day from libraries

LIBRARY CO-OPERATION

in the area wishing to borrow books which are not in their own stock. The cost—estimated at £200 a year—of the upkeep of the Bureau will be met by small subscriptions from the co-operating libraries.

The second fully organised Regional System to be established is that for the West Midland counties of Hereford, Shropshire, Stafford, Warwick, and Worcester. In this case the Birmingham Public Library is acting as the Regional Library Bureau. The general organisation is the same as that for the four Northern counties, though the number of libraries to be dealt with is considerably larger. The West Midland Bureau commenced work on April 1, 1931.

The county which may claim the honour of having established the pioneer Regional Library System is Cornwall, though, owing to the small number of libraries in the county and the absence of any large library, it has not developed on the scale of the Northern or the West Midland groups. In 1927 seven of the nine urban libraries and the County Library agreed to co-operate. A union catalogue has been compiled and is housed at the County Library, which acts as the Regional Bureau.

A special committee was appointed at the Conference of Welsh Library Authorities in May 1931 to organise a Regional System for the whole of Wales. It is proposed that a union catalogue should be housed at the National Library of Wales, which library will act as the Regional Bureau. A duplicate of that section of the catalogue which covers South

Wales and Monmouthshire (which area contains most of the large libraries in Wales) will be housed in the Cardiff Public Library.

The Departmental Committee appointed to report on the library provision in Northern Ireland has recommended that a Regional Scheme be adopted for the whole of Northern Ireland, and that a new State Library, at which the Regional Bureau would be housed, should be established. In London a union catalogue (on cards) of the non-fiction books in the libraries of the Metropolitan Boroughs and the Guildhall Library is being compiled and is being housed at the National Central Library.

It will be seen from the details just given that there is every likelihood of about one-third of the total area of England and Wales being served by Regional Schemes within the next two or three years, and it is possible that within the next decade the whole country will be served by ten or a dozen Regional Groups, each with its own Bureau and union catalogue. The great advantage of these Regional Groups is that by pooling their books the co-operating libraries are mobilising innumerable books which would otherwise lie idle on their shelves, the result being that the demand made on the National Central Library is considerably reduced, thus making it possible for the latter to use its all too small book fund for the purchase of books which would otherwise be unobtainable.

If the Regional Schemes are to function satisfactorily it is necessary that there should be some insti-

LIBRARY CO-OPERATION

tution which provides liaison between the various Regional Bureaux, and which acts as a great national reserve for books which are not obtainable in the Regional Areas. This need is met by the National Central Library (formerly the Central Library for Students), the main functions of which are: (*a*) to lend otherwise unobtainable books to libraries in Great Britain and Ireland; (*b*) to lend books to organised groups of adult students; (*c*) to act as a clearing-house for the loan of books in the libraries associated with it (known as Outlier Libraries); (*d*) to act as a liaison department between the various Regional Bureaux when they are established; (*e*) to form a union catalogue of the books in the Outlier Libraries; (*f*) to trace the whereabouts of copies of scarce books; (*g*) to supply bibliographical information; (*h*) to act as the National Centre for Bibliographical Information in Great Britain, in association with similar centres which have been, or are being, established in other countries.

The libraries in England which have no Regional Bureaux deal direct with the National Central Library, those in Wales send their applications through the National Library of Wales, those in Scotland through the Scottish Central Library for Students at Dunfermline, and those in Ireland through the Irish Central Library for Students at Dublin. These three libraries forward to the National Central Library those applications they are unable to deal with themselves. The Central Library does not supply fiction, the ordinary text-books required by students in connection with examinations, books which are in print costing less than six shillings, and books which the local library should buy for itself. It does not lend books direct to readers, but only through the local public, university, or other library to which they have access: the reason for this being (*a*) that the stock of the local library is drawn on first, and (*b*) that the reader is educated to look upon his local library as his natural source for the supply of books. In other words, the Central Library does not interfere with the legitimate work of the local library. No charge, other than the cost of postage both ways, is made for the loan of books.

One of the most important functions of the Central Library is that dealing with the Outlier Libraries. An Outlier Library is one which undertakes to lend its books to any other library through the agency of the National Central Library. At the end of 1930 there were 108 Outlier Libraries, with a total stock of nearly four and a half million volumes, including some 26,000 sets of periodicals. For a list of these libraries, see the current Annual Report of the National Central Library.

In addition to the union catalogues of the Outlier Libraries and the London Borough Libraries, copies of the union catalogues of each of the Regional Bureaux will be housed at the National Central Library. It is possible, therefore, that in the course of the next few years a great national union catalogue of the books in most of the libraries in Great

LIBRARY CO-OPERATION

Britain and Ireland will be available and will form one of the most valuable bibliographical tools in the world. It is to assist in this work that the Regional Bureaux are adopting sheaf catalogues, rather than card catalogues, for their union catalogues. A carbon copy of each slip will be forwarded to the National Central Library.

Lack of space precludes details of many other minor—though important and instructive—forms of co-operation, such as the work which the Joint Standing Committee on Library Co-operation is doing for the university libraries; the many schemes of co-operation between small urban libraries and their county library; inter-lending of books and inter-availability of readers' tickets between small groups of urban libraries; and co-operation between small groups of neighbouring libraries in the purchase of expensive books. Students wishing to have information on these and other forms of library co-operation should consult the following books:—

Report of the Departmental Committee on Public Libraries, 1927. *Chapter V deals with co-operation between neighbouring libraries, regional libraries, and the central library.*

Report of the Departmental Committee on Libraries in Northern Ireland, 1929.

The Annual Reports of the Carnegie United Kingdom Trust.

The Annual Reports of the National Central Library (formerly the Central Library for Students).

County Libraries Reports. Published annually by the Library Association.

A PRIMER OF LIBRARIANSHIP

The chapter on Co-operation in "The Year's Work in Librarianship," published annually by the Library Association.

The article on "The Future of the Central Library for Students" on pages 169–94 of the Proceedings of the Fiftieth Anniversary Conference of the Library Association, 1928.

WARNER (JOHN). Reference Library Methods, 1928. *Chapter XI deals with "Inter-library loans," and Chapter XII with "Other means of co-operation."*

CHAPTER XV

COMMERCIAL AND TECHNICAL LIBRARIES

BY GEORGE HALSALL

Librarian, Commercial Reference Library, Liverpool Public Libraries

The Commercial and Technical Library is established for the benefit of those concerned in buying, or selling, or manufacturing to sell. Its function is to provide, and have readily available, the latest reliable information upon such sections of commerce and industry as affect the locality which the library serves. Not only should the use of its resources facilitate everyday business transactions, but it should also help to discover possibilities of extending the area of business operations. Public Commercial Libraries have been in operation a sufficient length of time to prove that this ideal is practicable.

This kind of library should be established in the main Reference Library premises, provided that this building is placed in or near the commercial heart of the city, and that facilities exist for the concentration of the commercial stock, and the separation of this busy quarter from the non-business or student section of the Reference Library. If unavoidably housed in a Reference Library that is inconveniently distant from the commercial "beat," special telephonic communication will be necessary in addition to other provisions for giving ready response to hurried business enquiries.

The commercial library which is housed in a separate establishment entails two obvious disadvantages: duplication of certain stock and the loss to business men of more resources of the reference department than could possibly be withdrawn for Commercial Library purposes. The stock will vary with the special purpose of the library and the business needs of the locality, inland manufacturing places specialising on all matters technical, with the distribution and export side following up; while raw materials, transport, prices, customs duties, etc., will form the specialities of the Commercial Library situated on the sea-board.

Certain classes of commercial and technical works are of service in most commercial libraries wherever situated. Roughly grouped, these will consist of encyclopædias, both of a general kind and of particular branches of business and industry, such as accountancy, banking, chemical technology, business practice, law, etc. Year-books, British and foreign; trade directories; trade periodicals; foreign technical and commercial dictionaries; rates of exchange; railway time-tables; goods classification schedules; railway rate-books; motor-coach and aerial time-tables; maps, atlases, and gazetteers; customs procedure and tariffs; telegraphic codes and cable addresses; Government publications affecting commerce and trade, including the Board of Trade and Department of Overseas Trade Reports and

COMMERCIAL AND TECHNICAL LIBRARIES

statistics; trade catalogues; patent specifications and trade-marks (where space permits), and commercial text-books representative of the many ramifications of commerce and industry; advertising; salesmanship; market analysis; stamp duties; registration of business names; commercial and maritime law dealing with carriage of goods by land and sea; contracts; sale of goods; company law; patent and trade-mark laws, etc. Special attention should be paid to the provision of telegraphic codes, which are indispensable aids to commercial communication. The chief needs of localities are met by codes suitable to their particular industries.

Open access, with ample shelf-edge labels indicating the subjects contained upon the shelves, and bold standard subject-headings and number-guides are advisable. The classification in general use appears to be Dewey's, but there is no doubt that a special collection should receive special classification, one giving simple class-letters and an individualisation to each book by a different number.

The catalogue may well be compiled on the dictionary principle of author, title, and subject. With elaborate indexing this method gives every satisfaction.

Atlases and gazetteers are in constant use, and the best and latest should be obtained. Large-scale roller maps of the countries of the world are a necessity. Equally essential are large-scale road maps, population density, or zone maps; railways, canals, and product areas; coal-field, timber, etc.

Directory maps should be kept in alphabetical order in special boxes and not left in the directories. Large, straight brass hat-hooks (curved upwards at the end) screwed two abreast on a wall or partition make cheap and effective appliances for storing roller-maps, or they may be folded or made to be drawn like blinds on spring-rollers.

A selection of the chief national and local commercial and financial papers should be available in such numbers as may be required. Any matter in them not commercial should be extracted or blotted out, otherwise the general and non-commercial reader will be attracted, and his visits will detrimentally affect the library service to the hurried commercial consultant. Where shipping papers are taken it is advisable to extract the sailing lists and affix them to a separate board or stand; they are thus always on view and may be used by several readers simultaneously. For this purpose two copies of the paper will be needed.

The simplest and most effective method of dealing with trade catalogues, which are valuable guides to British (or foreign) manufactures, is to give them accession numbers, and, to cope as well as possible with the familiar difficulty of size-variation, store them in folio boxes which bear clearly indicated the accession numbers of their contents. Entries in two sheaf (or card) catalogues, one giving the names of firms and the other the names of articles manufactured, afford an easy clue to the desired article.

When the Commercial Library is separated from

COMMERCIAL AND TECHNICAL LIBRARIES

the Reference Library considerations of space may prevent patent specifications and trade-marks from forming part of the stock, or limits them to the Abridgement Series and the Illustrated Journal. Under any circumstance books on the law relating to patents and trade-marks, and also H.M. Stationery Office published guides for patentees, etc., should be obtained.

Trade periodicals constitute one of the most vital sections of a commercial library's stock, for they give the latest word on their respective subjects. Strict punctuality regarding their arrival is imperative, particularly of the daily market reports and the Customs Bills of Entry, if such are included in the stock of periodicals.

It is wise to start the collection of these publications with standard commercial journals and a small additional selection of others dealing with the known industries of the locality. Further guidance will be afforded by the repeated demands of the users of the library.

The value of a commercial periodical should be tested from time to time by withdrawing it from its case in the rack, placing inside the case a notice that the periodical in question is available on application.

For the display of periodicals the display-rack known as the "toast-rack" is both convenient and economical of space. The cases are placed on edge, with the rack number and the title of the magazine printed lengthwise on the spine. A grading of group sizes, with all possible classification of subject within each size, should be effected. Careless replacing of magazines by readers may be checked by having the different size-groups differentiated by various coloured cases. With both size and colour enlisted in the cause of order a double "jolt" is given to the careless replacer. After rack service the subsequent placing on the reference file demands strict attention, for reference to back numbers is constantly made. An alphabetical filing arrangement by title is more satisfactory than a numerical one by rack number.

For filing information extracted from the periodicals, or other sources, the vertical method finds favour, and certain of its advantages are too obvious to question, particularly where little binding of periodicals is done, or where filing space is too limited to permit of storage of parts for any lengthy period. Great care is, however, necessary that periodicals which should not suffer mutilation are not included in the risky process exercised in vertical filing. Needless to state, it requires constant revision and replacement or the files soon become other than an up-to-date aid.

Much of the routine work is similar to that of the reference library: indeed, commercial library work may truly be described as reference library principles functioning further along the lines of research, and focused upon two special subjects—Commerce and Industry. The business community have, very naturally, invested the title "Commercial

COMMERCIAL AND TECHNICAL LIBRARIES

Library" with a potentiality of aid greater than that which they attached to the title "Reference Library." The Public Library Movement having created this greater expectation must, by mobilising the valuable matter contained in the stocks of commercial libraries, transform the library into a clearing-house of commercial information. Nothing can do this but indexing, intensive and extensive. That which is not palpable must be disclosed; scattered facts must be brought together, ready for swift delivery. The business man can ill afford, in business hours, either to wait or search for information. Practical evidence of this was soon forthcoming at the Liverpool Commercial Reference Library after its opening in August 1917, and, guided by the "constant requirements," the following indexes were compiled. They are suitable for most commercial libraries.

Special Indexes

Periodicals' Contents.—A list of the established features of the commercial and industrial periodicals, reports, etc. These analyticals may well be set out in double-columned folio sheets displayed in a frame near the racks, the contents forming one alphabetical sequence of country and subject. It should be possible for each sheet to be withdrawn for alteration or additions with but little trouble. The fact of having "on sight" all magazines containing anything bearing upon their special subject gives keen satisfaction to the men of business, for they of all people prefer to look at facts rather than search for them. Supplementary to the above, daily notes should be taken by the Commercial Librarian of the more important current matters (other than the established features) which he meets in his reading of commercial periodicals and reports. Such work carries over until the appearance of the printed indexes of these periodicals.

Customs Tariffs Changes.—Customs tariffs are subject to such frequent changes that full reliance can hardly be placed on any annual statement regarding them. Kelly's great guide ceased publication in 1925. *The Shipping World Year-Book* continues, but suffers the limitations of an annual, and it deals only with British Empire tariffs. The Board of Trade fortunately lists the changes weekly in its ever-useful Journal, and the commercial library, by maintaining a consolidated alphabet of these, makes patent all current changes under the respective countries and subjects affected. Upon publication of the special consolidated tariff issues of the *Board of Trade Journal* the entries concerned are removed from this index.

Legislation Affecting Commerce Abroad.—These alterations (other than tariff changes) in commercial laws are collected from authentic sources, such as the Journals and Reports of the Chambers of Commerce of various districts, and from the *Journal of Comparative Legislation and International Law*, quarterly. Without claiming to be a complete survey of all changes effected in the respective coun-

COMMERCIAL AND TECHNICAL LIBRARIES

tries, this index has on numerous occasions proved its value as a supplementary list to the published decrees and commercial laws.

Trade Brands and Names.—This index is compiled from the latest advertisements in the trade journals. It is particularly useful when the commercial library, through separation from the main reference library, or through lack of space to house the Patent Specifications and Trade Marks section, has to rely upon its own resources for this type of information.

Supplementary Gazetteer.—Gathered with special care from authentic sources, this is a collection of place-names not given in gazetteers. It has solved many geographical difficulties occasioned by variations in the spelling of place-names abroad, and has localised places formerly considered too obscure for entry in printed gazetteers, but which, evidently, are now sufficiently prosperous to send orders for British goods. The queries which have caused the search for their locality have generally been for the port nearest to them.

Telegraphic Addresses Abroad. — The countries which publish their registered telegraphic addresses are all too few, and to the business world this lack has often occasioned serious worry and delay. It very frequently happens that our business firms receive communications for the first time from some unknown foreign firm, and the only identity provided is an undiscoverable cable address. The published registers are augmented by listing the cable addresses often given in the foreign Chambers of Commerce annual reports, and from advertisements, as found in foreign commercial magazines.

Maps.—This index incorporates with the set of roller maps all other maps in the library books and directories.

Trade Directories.—The contents of these are set out in two alphabets under locality and subject of manufacture. The chief cities and towns are selected for entry.

Economic Products.—From books, trade and other commercial journals, information is constantly being sought and collected respecting new raw materials or products, their places of origin, their analysis and discovered uses. Newly discovered uses for by-products and old raw materials are also noted in this index.

This being but an outline sketch of the constitution and conduct of the commercial library, only a summary of the salient features is here attempted. The masses are grouped, and to a larger Manual[1] must be left the filling in of details. It may, however, be noted that every activity stated in the foregoing account has been called into being by definitely manifested needs of the class which the commercial library is intended to serve. By the aid of library science the commercial library can now reveal to the business man many items of profitable information. This fact is well known where commercial libraries

---

[1] *Manual of Commercial and Technical Libraries*, by S. A. Pitt. Published by Messrs. George Allen & Unwin and the Library Association.

COMMERCIAL AND TECHNICAL LIBRARIES

have been in operation, and such knowledge has reacted so strongly upon business sentiment that a much more tolerant acceptance of the library rate now obtains than formerly. The business man has accepted the commercial library as an ally, realising that the old-time sources of information are no longer adequate for him; that he has now to seek business, and dare not risk being ill-informed as to opportunities to extend it. The commercial library when fulfilling its purpose becomes, indeed, a reflection of current events in the business world. Upon this fact the business man is becoming accustomed to rely.

THE MAIN USES OF THE COMMERCIAL AND TECHNICAL LIBRARY

The most practical manner in which these can be manifested is by a list of "constants" in the way of readers' requirements.

These illustrative examples, drawn from the actual, will also, in a measure, indicate the quality of stock requisite to meet such needs. For some fourteen years variations of these inquiries have formed quite a large part of the day's work in the Liverpool Commercial Library, and as both Commerce and Industry receive attention there, the following may be taken as typical business requirements:—

Trade openings at home and abroad; contracts open, etc.
Business addresses of merchants, shippers, manufacturers, importers and exporters, agents, etc.
Telegraphic cable coding and decoding.
Telegraphic addresses at home and abroad.
Daily, Weekly, and Monthly market reports on commercial commodities and raw materials. Their country of

origin, general, and newly discovered uses; statistics as to quantities imported or exported; prices current and at varying dates.

By-products from trade waste: their uses.

Chemical technology on various subjects: coal tars, dyes, etc.

Processes of the various industries: colour-making, tanning, rope-making, etc.

Rates of exchange foreign currencies; past dates, by the way, are used more frequently than current. The exchange rate file should be kept very near the enquiry desk.

Customs tariffs alterations abroad.

Shipping matters concern Business libraries, whether situated inland or on the coast, in the matter of import and export procedure. A fairly full list is here given: Particulars of ships from Shipping Registers: Lloyd's and others; current shipbuilding and repairs; new inventions of ships' gear; whereabouts of ships afloat; costs and other data of all classes of fuel; stowage and freight tables; customs procedure; classifications of dangerous cargoes and Board of Trade rules concerning them; sailing lists; distance tables; agents of steamship lines in home and foreign ports; dock and port charges and cargo-handling equipment of home and foreign ports; depths of water and widths of foreign rivers; nearest ports to certain obscure places abroad from which orders have been received for the first time; whereabouts of places not mentioned in gazetteers; current seasons for shipment of goods of special features abroad.

Costs of living, taxation, climate, etc., at different foreign places is often required by commercial travellers and those obtaining employment abroad.

Commercial (or business) codes obtaining in foreign countries.

Commercial and maritime laws: such as carriage of goods on land and sea; contracts; sale of goods; stamp duties; master and servant; agency law; trade marks and patent law; registration of business names.

COMMERCIAL AND TECHNICAL LIBRARIES

Insurance: life; marine; motor; fire risks regulations; dangerous cargo classifications.

Trade statistics and reports; Board of Trade returns and other Government publications, British and foreign, giving exports and imports; Chambers of Commerce Reports.

Trade Brands and Trade Marks on goods; manufacturers sought.

British Engineering Standard specifications of colours; oils; varnishes; building and engineering materials; coal tar products; dyes.

Weights and measures: specific gravity and bulk correspondences in English and foreign and metric measures.

Mercantile tables.

Questions on law changes affecting commerce and trade (British and foreign): Statutory Rules and Orders; Merchandise Marks; Merchant Shipping; food laws; packing; etc.

Health and Unemployment Insurance Acts; Workmen's Compensation; Factory Acts.

Taxation: plant and premises; questions of rating; income tax and super-tax.

Road Transport: motor haulage time and distance tables; particulars concerning varying makes of commercial cars, lorries, etc.

Railway rates and classifications; particulars of stations' equipment in cranes, etc.

Railway companies guides, time-tables, traffic-tables, personnel.

Population statistics: particulars showing buying habits and powers of various localities, to gauge possibilities of marketing certain products.

Companies; investments; reports of meetings; financial standing and personnel of firms.

Translations of foreign technical and commercial correspondence. (N.B.—A list of qualified translators with their business addresses is available.)

CHAPTER XVI

BUSINESS LIBRARIES

BY B. M. HEADICAR, F.L.A.

Librarian of the London School of Economics and Political Science. Lecturer on Library Organisation at the School of Librarianship

The business library, or information bureau, is a modern introduction, and only in quite recent years has it grown to large numbers. Even now it is not a general feature of business in this country, but it is growing gradually in favour, while in the United States there are probably ten thousand business libraries in operation, most of which have been instituted since the war ended. The business man, to be successful, must know at least as much as his keenest competitor. He has no longer the time to spare to hunt up his own information, unless he is prepared to fall behind in the race for orders. The public commercial library obviously cannot specialise on the needs of an individual business man, so it is essential for the latter to provide for his special requirements by having at his disposal sources of information regarding every aspect of his particular commercial concern. The public commercial library has to cater for every business and for commerce as a whole. The business man requires his information exact and full, at the moment of asking. The business library is a vital necessity to every firm desiring to be progressive. It is equally

BUSINESS LIBRARIES

essential that a qualified librarian should be in charge of such a library. The trained librarian knows "how." How to collect and arrange material, how to serve it up, how to preserve and how and when to discard. His first duties will be to arrange for the centralisation in his department of all information, printed and written, within the establishment itself, and secondly to tabulate the other sources of information in libraries and institutions within his area, and to arrange for the fullest co-operation with them all.

The business library is not usually concerned with books as such in large numbers, but with the mass of periodical literature and newspaper clippings which are so essential to keep the library up to date. Such books as are needed will be mostly reference books, directories, gazetteers, code books, statistical annuals, year-books of Chambers of Commerce, with such ordinary treatises as are of value to the immediate needs of the establishment. Maps, trade catalogues, photographs, lantern slides may all be necessary, the need varying according to the type of business concerned. Books should be classified on the Decimal System; there is no need for the business librarian to try and devise a system of his own. He will probably get anything but satisfactory results if he does. Besides, why try to do again what has already been well done by some of the world's greatest experts. Maps, trade catalogues, photographs, and lantern slides, will all be required to be kept each in a separate classification. There is no reason why any of these should be entered in an accession book or similar register. The business man is not keen on statistics of a stock which is ever varying. The catalogue can meet all requirements in this direction.

Each volume received should be stamped with the firm's name immediately on receipt, and a copy of the accounts for all books purchased should be kept in the library. A subject entry of the book should be made for the alphabetical catalogue, and for this purpose the Library of Congress List of Subject Headings or one of the other ready prepared lists should be used to avoid the use of synonymous headings. In many cases it will be found that the subject list does not cover the very specific headings required to meet the needs of a particular business. The librarian, therefore, must acquaint himself thoroughly with the terminology used by the firm and make such additions to his list as may be necessary in order to get the most specific heading in common use. Always keep the list of headings, whether printed or written, at hand, and make sure that any heading you use bears the same meaning as that understood in the business itself. Any work classified should have its classification number carried on to the back of the title-page and a gummed label (Dennison's A65 is a very suitable size) should be attached to the back of each volume, and the same number entered upon the label. Remember to damp the gummed label both sides. Many of the complaints about these labels coming off are due to the neglect of this practice.

BUSINESS LIBRARIES

Periodicals are usually the chief basis for acquiring up-to-date information, and some businesses take a very considerable number. Most progressive firms advertise freely in trade journals and voucher copies of all of these are usually sent to all advertisers. When a periodical arrives it should at once be marked off on the usual periodical card, and should then be stamped with the firm's name or library stamp. One of the most important tasks of the librarian is to see to the proper "routing" of periodicals. This "routing" consists in the regular dispatch of the periodical to the persons most intimately concerned with its contents, not only to provide information for the reader, but in order that any article of special or permanent importance may be indicated. The article is then either cut out and placed for preservation in the vertical file, or, if the periodical is one which is permanently kept and bound, an entry is made for it in the alphabetical index. To ensure that "routing" is properly carried out, a list of the persons who require to read a periodical is entered on the back of the periodical card, in the order in which each person is to receive the issue. The old method of pasting a slip with these names upon it on the cover of the periodical, leaving each person the task of handing the periodical to the next person on the list is not satisfactory. In most cases the first individual forgets to hand the periodical on until far too late, or else he either omits to do it altogether or declares he has done so, while number two is just as clear he has never received the issue in question. The only safe plan is for the librarian himself to be responsible for the delivery of the periodical and for its collection in each case.

When a volume of a periodical is complete it should be bound in a good buckram if it is required for permanent reference. Wherever possible, the advertisement sheets should be removed before binding. This reduces the cost of binding and saves a lot of space on the shelves. Those not required to be kept permanently should be retained as long as needed and then discarded, care being taken that all articles marked as important during "routing" have been removed for preservation. Keep in touch with the public library and ensure that no periodical is thrown away if it is likely to be of service to the general reader and that the public library is prepared to find a home for it. In many cases the library will be glad of the opportunity.

Pamphlets and clippings are of the greatest importance in the business library, but to be of full service they must be carefully and methodically arranged, so that instant use can be made of them when required, and that a specific place is reserved for them when not in use. Pamphlets should be kept in the vertical file, the ideal method of keeping such material, newspaper cuttings, and similar documents. The vertical file consists of manila folders and guides, kept upright in a set of drawers or cabinets, and arranged in systematic order. Each folder has its subject marked on its projecting edge, and the printed and other small material concerned

BUSINESS LIBRARIES

with that subject is dropped into the folder as received, having first entered upon it the name of the subject corresponding to that on the folder. No attempt need be made to keep any definite order within the folder itself. The most suitable vertical file is what is called the legal size, each drawer measuring 10½ in. high, 15¼ in. wide, and 24 in. deep (inside measurements). Whether metal or wood files are used is largely a matter of taste. Wood usually appeals to the person of an æsthetic mind, but it is now generally more expensive, takes up more room, and is more inflammable. Steel drawers are cheaper, and when a large number is in use, a considerable amount of floor space is saved, owing to the thinness of the material compared to wood. In fact, rather more than half an inch of space is saved with each unit. On the other hand, many people complain that the metal file becomes noisy in use after a time, however good the make may be. Folders, about 14 in. by 9 in., should allow expansion of about 1 in., and the front-edge should be half an inch shorter than the back. In large collections it is advisable to have guide cards with tabs in three divisions and also in files with the material geographically arranged and then subdivided by subject. The alphabetical arrangement of the file material is simple, straightforward, requires little cataloguing, is easily understood, and convenient for instant reference without previous consultation of catalogues or indexes to classifications.

An alphabetical catalogue to the whole collection

is required, but need only contain references under subjects and not individual entries for every pamphlet, etc., in the library. Author entries should be given for all treatises and to pamphlets of outstanding importance. A series card should also be made for numbered series, such as, for instance, the publications of the Empire Marketing Board, but it is not necessary to give full details. All that is required is to enter the number of each publication, the title, and the subject-heading under which it will be found in the vertical file. Large numbers of cuttings should be kept in a large envelope behind the folder, while those of permanent value should be mounted on a U-file-um strip. This is a gummed strip which is stuck inside the folder. Each strip contains about 30–40 gummed tabs. The cutting is attached top and bottom to one of these tabs and is made secure from loss when used. Many cuttings can be mounted on each strip and several strips will easily be taken if required in each folder. Be sure that each cutting bears the source and date of issue upon it. Without such information cuttings are valueless. The greater part of this vertical file material will require to be kept for long periods, containing as it does most of the facts upon which the business man will have to rely, but a certain amount will have quite an ephemeral value, hence the librarian should be careful to discard any out-of-date matter whenever he has to put new matter in the files, whilst at least once a year a systematic search through the folders should be made and all pamphlets and cuttings which have been superseded by later information should be turned out. This work of elimination is an important task as, unless it is thoroughly and carefully done, not only is there undue accumulation, but there is always the risk of someone being given out-of-date information. The same golden rule—when in doubt retain—applies to this material just as forcibly as it does to the question of discarding in any public library.

Separate catalogues of maps, slides, trade catalogues, photographs, etc., may be desirable. It will depend largely upon the character of the business. All maps likely to be in frequent use should be mounted on linen, kept flat in drawers, and arranged geographically. An important point to remember in regard to periodicals subscribed for is to draw a line on the catalogue checking card in front of the month when the subscription expires and three months ahead in the case of a periodical coming from a long distance. This serves as a reminder that the subscription requires renewal and should be sent off in good time to ensure there is no interruption in the supply.

The cost of a business library is mainly concerned with staff and equipment. If a room is provided in premises already rented floor space will cost nothing. The salary of the librarian and his assistants and clerical staff will be the heaviest charge. This will vary according to the size of the establishment. Vertical files (two-drawer cabinet) of the size mentioned above can be purchased for

£7 10s. in steel. Excellent shelving for the purpose is the metal kind named "Steeletta," a standard case, 7 ft. 6 in. by 3 ft. by 8 in., costing about £3. It is adjustable to one inch and is the cheapest good shelving in metal I have met with. Having used it I can recommend it. Cards 5 in. by 3 in. should be used for the catalogue. Good quality cards can be obtained for 6s. per 1,000. Remember that indexes which do not get much handling can very well be kept on stiff paper slips instead of cards. They cost about one-fourth the price of cards and take infinitely less room, thus reducing considerably the expenditure on cabinets. Folders and guide cards cost very little. A table for reading, 6 ft. by 3 ft, and a desk can probably be provided from the furniture already in the establishment.

Finally, let me again emphasise the need of appointing a qualified librarian. He will not only understand the technique of librarianship but he will necessarily have reached an educational standard which will make it easy for him soon to become saturated with the commercial details of the business, to understand the special aspects of it attached to various members of the staff, to sense beforehand the information likely to be of value to each, to gain the complete confidence of all, and so make his library what it can easily be, an indispensable and vital department.

CHAPTER XVII

LIBRARY PUBLICATIONS

BY J. P. LAMB
Chief Librarian of the Sheffield Public Libraries

Most library publications are intended to serve one or more of the following purposes:

1. To be general guides to the contents of the library.
2. To guide readers desirous of undertaking courses of reading in various subjects.
3. To interest the general reader (and more particularly the novel reader) in certain books or subjects.
4. To attract non-users to the library.

A wide range of method is employed for the attainment of these four objects; but within the limits of this chapter it is only possible to deal with a few of the more important types of library publications in general use.

It is an axiom that the best publicity is service; common sense therefore argues that the library service must be able to cope with any demand upon it that publicity may create.

It is as well not to issue a library publication without having in view a precise object, which will determine the design of the publication and its method of distribution. Books, cataloguing method, format, approach and distribution should all have a definite relation to reader and purpose; and the librarian should analyse the results of his methods as carefully and scientifically as the commercial advertising expert.

Complete printed library catalogues are now rarely produced, but sectional class catalogues, dealing with the more popular classes, are still issued. The general tendency, however, is to compile catalogues which are selective in the choice of books and of limited objective as regards the public they serve. This type of select catalogue can deal with a particular trade, profession, or industry, or a general grouping of subjects designed to meet the needs of large classes of general readers.

Such catalogues are comparatively cheap to produce; they can therefore be prepared for gratuitous circulation in large numbers, and their distribution made to serve a wider purpose than that of a mere record of books on certain subjects for actual library users. Those lists which deal with trades and professions, for instance, will reach large numbers of non-readers by issue through trade unions, employers' organisations, and professional bodies to their members.

Select catalogues intended for non-readers must *attract* readers to the library and to books. To accomplish this the format must be arresting; it is advisable to decide on a size not exceeding $8\frac{1}{2}$ in. by $5\frac{1}{2}$ in., which is handy for the pocket; an illustrated cover in colour compels attention. The use of books is aided by annotations simply and brightly written; the academic style suitable for a reference library catalogue is clearly out of place in such a production. Illustrations add greatly to appearance and interest. The insides of the cover pages can be used with advantage for notices of library activities likely to appeal to the users of the catalogue. These notes should be bold and brief; massed printing is quite useless for matter of this kind.

A select children's catalogue should move even further from normal methods of catalogue production. If attractiveness is desirable for adults, it is essential for children, and there is much to be said for making the selection of books, the choice of type, paper and cover, and the use of verses, illustrations, and subject-headings which interpret the child mind, serve this general purpose. The grouping of stories under subject-headings is a help to children, parents, and teachers, in encouraging the acquisition of "facts without tears." As simplicity in terminology and arrangement is implicit in a children's catalogue, the librarian should consider whether the acknowledged clarity of the dictionary form is a factor that can be ignored.

One important advantage of a select catalogue is that it can be given a definite life by including only books which may reasonably be expected to escape the regular processes of discarding.

The majority of library publications are bibliographies or select reading lists. The average public library is concerned primarily with the general reader, and the object of most "aids" is to interest him in reading books which he would normally disregard; it is assumed that the advanced reader is familiar with the literature of his subject. Readers' aids may conveniently be divided into two groups—specialist and popular. The word specialist is used to denote publications designed for general readers who want guidance either in a specific subject or a group of related subjects; the popular aid is intended for the reader who reads casually or limits himself to fiction.

The first problem that confronts the librarian preparing a series of specialist aids is to decide whether to enlist the services of an expert or to rely on his own and his staff's book knowledge. Professional prestige is gained by the library if the staff does the work; on the other hand, few public librarians can find sufficient time for reading to allow them to write a critical evaluation of the literature of any subject. An expert gives authority to the list; and the use of his name has considerable publicity value. On the whole, provided that experts who have the right approach to the lay mind can be obtained, it is advisable to have their assistance.

The general style of the publication must next be considered. It may be an annotated list of books in two or three groups, leading from elementary to more advanced works; or the books may be discussed in a short article which outlines the subject and evaluates the books as they occur in relation to

LIBRARY PUBLICATIONS

the points made. This latter is clearly the better form to adopt, as, if interest can be stimulated, the reader falls more readily into a prescribed course of reading. To facilitate reference it is advisable to reprint the titles of the books recommended in a plain list at the end of the pamphlet.

The purpose of the aid will be furthered by brevity. Two thousand words is ample for the article; large subjects can be dealt with sectionally. Format is important; pocket size is advocated for all such publications. It is to be emphasised that the cover should be compelling; a bold illustration and colour printing give variety and make the list noticeable. The type selected should be of reasonable size and artistic design; a good type costs no more than a poor one. A ten-point type is a useful size for the body of the article; with the lines well leaded, and, with good margins, an attractive page is produced. It is advisable to emphasize titles mentioned in the text by the use of a different type. For the list of books recommended an eight-point type is sufficient; but the choice of this will depend on the length of the completed pamphlet, as it is sometimes necessary to use smaller or larger type in order to obtain the right number of pages to allow stapling in series of four pages. The inside of the cover can be used for notices of library activities.

As it is impossible to gauge precisely the reading standard of the public to be served, and the best means of approach to that standard, a specialist aid should cover a reasonably wide range of reading, commencing with elementary books and finally reaching a fairly advanced standard. Care should be taken to avoid in the introductory part the inclusion of books which might repel by reason of turgidity of style or academic treatment; too often is the expert unable to reach the outlook of the common man. There is fortunately a large and growing literature on many subjects which ideally combines erudition with simplicity of treatment.

Distribution can be made through the libraries and through the secretaries of study groups, Adult School classes, W.E.A. classes, etc., which are studying the subject.

Specialist aids are issued regularly by many libraries either separately or in the library bulletin, and in some cases in both ways.

Reading values vary considerably in different towns, and book approach must be varied accordingly; but before any attempt is made to produce popular aids of any kind, some evaluation of the mental quality of the library clientèle should be attempted. It is generally true that the widest contact between readers of this type and books comes through pleasure in reading, and later through interest in the practical value of books.

A popular aid, therefore, should catch the attention. Interest is aroused by the use of a current motive; a topic of the day, the death of some eminent person, a centenary celebration, the creation of a new laureate, or any event which has seized the popular imagination, can be pressed into the service of the library. Approach to larger groups can be made by lists on such subjects as sport, hobbies, home handicrafts, gardening, etc., for men; and dressmaking, cookery, housewifery, mothercraft, home decoration and furnishing, etc., for women. The barrier between fiction and non-fiction is a very real one to many library users who have a perfectly understandable objection to attempts being made to uplift them, and it is well worth while to make them realise that books can help them with practical problems of the normal workaday experience. There is also scope for the preparation of occasional popular lists in small broadside form on many subjects, of which the following are examples: "Modern drama"; "As salt as the sea: a selection of sea stories"; "Twenty-five books to read again and again": a selection of popular classics; "Seas and lands: thirty travel triumphs"; "New voices: modern essayists"; and so on.

Variety in size, shape, style, and colour of paper should be attempted; a simple descriptive annotation to each book should be given; and the number of books on the type of aid which has only the interest of a current event to popularise it should never exceed thirty. Very careful selection of "introductory" books is desirable. In subjects such as sports, cookery, etc., on which a heavy stock is presumably carried and for which there is always some regular reading demand, a "folder" list on thin card or stiff paper may be used with advantage; the form of the smaller list will vary according to the number of books dealt with. A convenient form is a folded leaflet with three pages of matter, the front page being left for title and a short provocative paragraph on the subject.

Many of the large library systems, and some of the more enterprising among the smaller, publish monthly, bi-monthly, or quarterly bulletins or library magazines distributed free or sold for a nominal sum. These serve as guides to current literature as represented in the library stocks; but they also include reading lists, notes on library activities, articles on outstanding books, local history, or other matters which will arouse interest in the library's work. A brightly written and well-produced bulletin is an important asset; it is possible to use it to establish friendly relations with the library public. Details of issues, exhibitions, lectures, the purpose of new regulations, and many other details of organisation help in the spread of that atmosphere of friendly contact between library and reader which it should be the aim of every librarian to create. The size of the bulletin will naturally depend on the funds at the librarian's disposal; its production is a costly item, and unless a bulletin is "alive" it fails to justify its upkeep. Suitable advertisements from local tradesmen will help to cover a proportion of the cost of production.

A specially-designed cover, the colour of which is varied with each issue, and occasional illustrations, add to its appeal. Publishers are usually willing to lend blocks to libraries for this purpose. It is

LIBRARY PUBLICATIONS

advisable to allot to a competent assistant the task of editing.

Printed bulletins for children are produced by a few libraries. The titles of two such bulletins are *The Chimney Corner* and *The Magic Casement*; both charmingly apt. An illustrated cover, large and well spaced print, and simple annotations are essential. Some American children's bulletins have delightful sketches among the text; illustrated matter is valuable if cost permits its inclusion.

Simple stories about books, events, and authors; selections of books on subjects of interest to children; additions to the children's libraries; and notices of lectures, programmes of story hours, seasonal festivities, etc., should be included. The editing of a children's bulletin is a difficult task, for children are keen critics, and the art of writing down without being ridiculously childish or offensively condescending is not easily acquired. The editing should be in the hands of a competent assistant with a wide experience of Children's Libraries.

Perhaps the most important of the many methods in use to bring non-readers to the library is the poster. Its appeal should be instant; a design in colour, with very few words, is the best for this purpose. Posters should be exhibited in clubs, workshops, welfare establishments, or any places where people congregate and the authorities are willing to display them.

CHAPTER XVIII

PRINT COLLECTING

BY J. L. DOUTHWAITE
Librarian of the Guildhall Library, London

To all those who are interested in the administration of our public libraries it is becoming increasingly apparent that, in addition to providing suitable books of reference and works of standard literature, it should also be considered as of equal importance to form a collection of prints and drawings illustrative primarily of the topography of the district of which the individual library may be the cultural centre. Such a collection will naturally include all maps and plans of the area, and it can be supplemented by portraits of historical and notable personages, and by representations of important events more or less associated with the special locality.

Assuming that the desirability of such collections has been realised, and that a certain amount of suitable material has been acquired, it will be evident that the necessity exists for a carefully thought out method of classifying and cataloguing the items. The suggestions which follow under these headings are based upon the measure of success which has attended the formation, more particularly during the last twenty years, of the print collection of the Library of the Corporation of London at Guildhall.

PRINT COLLECTING

The problems of the library situated in London and its suburbs are in many ways less formidable than those further afield. Here the proximity of the treasures of the British Museum, and the Victoria and Albert Museum, confines to narrow limits the work of education in art matters. In the provinces the centres of enlightenment have to be provided in all branches of learning, and the art of engraving, the progress of water-colours, and indeed all pictorial representation, must be considered as falling within the scope of the work expected. It naturally follows that my remarks are confined mainly to the problems which confront the districts likely to limit their activities to the formation of local collections.

A study, where possible, of the national possessions, is a splendid beginning. But it is amazing how little these collections are known, even by those who are generally well informed on such subjects. We all make our pilgrimages to Bloomsbury or South Kensington, but how many are familiar with the prints and drawings in the King's Library in the British Museum, or the English topographical water-colours in the Dixon bequest at Bethnal Green? Much of the contents of such collections is now unobtainable, but photographs of the items concerning the particular district in which the local library may be situated are well worthy of a place in its print collection. Neither the photograph nor the cutting from the illustrated paper should be despised. I am reminded how soon the former passes into the realm of historic interest by the receipt as a gift within the last few days from my good friend the City Librarian of Birmingham, of a photo taken by the late Sir Benjamin Stone of Lombard Street in 1902. Gone now are most of the frontages there depicted, and the costumes have, of course, passed out of knowledge. How historically valuable the despised woodcut from the illustrated paper becomes was shown when recently the Holborn Borough Council organised a most interesting local exhibition. Here cheek by jowl with a fine aquatint or a rich stipple was the crude woodcut from the penny paper or the early half-tone from an illustrated magazine; but all had their appropriate places and relative values.

The student of London topography should not neglect to examine the grangerised copy of Lyson's *Environs of London* in the Guildhall Library, with its special features of exquisite water-colours and carefully drawn armorial bearings; in many cases even the church monuments are drawn and the inscriptions copied, while the flora of the particular county is also illustrated. Mr. Philip A. Phillips has given a fine collection of topographical drawings to the London Museum; personally, I am sorry to see these relegated to the attics of Lancaster House, but the drawings are well worth climbing the staircase to see. Essex enthusiasts should study the Sage collection at Stoke Newington (particularly for information on Barking and district), and I direct the footsteps of the Surrey searcher to the

PRINT COLLECTING

Croydon Public Library; here the judicious patronage of the talents of the late Mr. Evacustes Phipson has resulted in the collection of a wealth of topographical material which would otherwise have inevitably been lost.

It is essential that some working knowledge should be obtained of the various processes of engraving, if the collection is to be built up on practical lines. And here let me utter a word of warning as to the futility of buying so-called proofs of process plates. Proofs generally are, I submit, much overrated; it is usually far better to buy the good print with title, line of publication, artist's and engraver's names, than to indulge in the purchase at an extravagant price of an earlier state of the plate which for public purposes is incomplete and like a book without a title-page. The word "proof" covers a multitude of issues—Engraver's proof, proof before letters, the etched or open-letter proof, and sometimes, unfortunately, false proof. The modern etching, aquatint, or mezzotint may be worthy of consideration in their early states, but no reasonable person can produce any argument for including, say, collotype or three-colour plates in the same category. And yet we see advertisements in respectable art journals offering these "signed artist's proofs" at enhanced prices, and the prospective patron is asked to believe that not only will he obtain an article of greater artistic merit, but that he will reap financial profit by the investment!

Careful and simple descriptions of the various

processes will be found indicated in the handbooks mentioned later on. Much may be learned from these, but there is a surer method of increasing knowledge, and that is to put your reading to the test—buy and burn your fingers! Only recently I noticed that a work just issued by an eminent firm of publishers contains almost every mistake possible in the descriptions of some of the prints illustrating the book; the mezzotint is dubbed the aquatint, prints are ascribed to wrong engravers, and others to artists who were innocent of any pictorial crime but that of painting. Do not let any guide to your district, which you may illustrate from the old engravings of the locality, contain such stupid blunders.

Much could be written of the other pitfalls which will dog the footsteps of the explorer in printland. An observant eye for the signs of the faker will do much to guard against the general imposture. Quite often the cupidity of the buyer is responsible for his downfall; the print is offered at much less than its market value, and in his haste to acquire it he is blinded to its defects.

The following simple precautions in examining prints or drawings will perhaps be of some use to the beginner; the first I have never seen mentioned in print, and few people realise its great value as a detector.

Examine the offered drawing or engraving at all angles, particularly upside down; this will readily reveal re-working on the plate, repairs in the paper or general touching-up which might otherwise escape detection. Look for the sign of applied dirt, which generally stops short of attacking the surface of the illustration. Try to choose daytime for your buying, and, if opportunity offers, closely inspect the proffered purchase by holding it in front of a strong light.

It is difficult to give any directions for the detection of the application of modern colouring to an old print. If the print has not been chemically cleaned, it will probably have colour applied *over* old fox-marks—a sure sign that it has passed through the faker's hand.

The Guildhall Library print collection is classified under the headings of the City Wards, with Westminster and Southwark divided into parishes; the streets are then arranged alphabetically as subdivisions with further headings as required. This seems to be a classification likely to be satisfactory for most districts. For those interested in a more detailed arrangement, the scheme recently formulated by Professor Leftwych for the Architectural Graphic Records Committee covers every possible point required, but it appears to be too elaborate for general adoption.

The catalogue slip, with the appropriate headings, such as:—

Cheap Ward. Cheapside. St. Mary-le-Bow

will give the title of the item, with artist's and engraver's name, the class of illustrations (watercolour, mezzotint, line, aquatint, etc.) with the measurement of the size of the actual drawing or engraving (ignoring in the latter plate line or margin). Two sizes of mounts for storage are recommended, viz. Royal (20 in. by 25 in.) and Imperial (22 in. by 32 in.); these should be "four-sheet" boards or stout cartridge paper; the former permits the use of hinges of jaconet for the items. These are easily detachable without injury to the illustration or the mount—an important point when frequent removals have to be made from the mounts. The hinges are only attached to the top edge of the print or drawing, bent back and fastened with paste along each edge. The mounts should be lettered at the top right-hand corner showing the same divisions as on the slip. For facility in finding, some index number (we adopt the pages of the printed catalogue of the collection) should be attached to the extreme bottom right-hand edge of mount. The mounts should be stored in boxes, of a type specially designed to exclude dust, lettered in accordance with the catalogue divisions. For portraits no better method can be devised than that adopted in the printed catalogue of the British Museum collections; the entries there are as concise as possible without leaving out any essential details.

A most admirable help to the study of prints is entitled: *A Guide to the Processes and Schools of Engraving*, by Professor Arthur M. Hind (1923); Singer and Strang on *Etching, Engraving and other methods of Printing Pictures* (1897) is invaluable, and the various methods of handling and cleaning prints are admirably dealt with in *Print Restoration and Picture Cleaning*, by M. J. Gunn (1911).

In addition to purely topographical subjects, there are various classes of printed matter once possibly despised, but now regarded as Rariora by collectors. Trade cards and engraved advertisements have now come into their own, and the 1,200 specimens of watchmakers' labels in the Library here is probably by far the largest in existence. Theatrical bills and programmes form another class of accessions which will certainly afford interest to future students. In conclusion, it may be remarked that whether the collector of to-day confines his attention to one class of prints or to various kinds, proper classification and indexing are the only means of preventing the specimens gathered together being anything else but a chaotic heap.

CHAPTER XIX

BINDING FOR LIBRARIES

BY DOUGLAS COCKERELL

It is only in the English-speaking countries that the general run of books is issued in cloth cases; elsewhere librarians have to get practically all the books they receive bound before they are put on the library shelves. In England there is always a question as to whether a book should or should not be re-bound, and in practice many books are left with such slight protection as is given by the ordinary publisher's covers.

The ordinary publisher's cloth case will not serve to protect books that have much use, especially if the volumes are heavy. This is largely because the connection between the case and the book is weak, but also because the covering material is poor. These defects are not inherent in publishers' bindings which, with a very little additional expense, can be made reasonably serviceable. At least one publisher in this country and several in America have issued some portion of their books strongly cased for library use, and these specially strengthened books have been found to be quite satisfactory, provided that the paper on which they are printed is sound.

By sewing on tapes, strengthening the endpapers, guarding plates, using a cloth with some strength in the basic weaving, and good boards, publishers can make their books capable of withstanding hard wear. The extra factory cost of the strengthened bindings is not high, but it must be remembered that in the ordinary publishing trade the actual production costs are multiplied by three at least to arrive at the selling-price of the book, so that the addition, say, of fourpence to the cost of binding generally means an added cost of at least one shilling to the retail purchaser.

But in spite of this there is no doubt that, if the publishers could be induced to issue important books really strongly bound, it would benefit the libraries to pay an additional price for books that would serve their need without rebinding.

The serviceability of a book which is subject to hard wear does not depend entirely or even mainly upon the strength of the binding; the nature and strength of the paper is a factor to be considered. Some paper, such as the soft woolly stuff known as "bulking paper," cannot be bound securely because the sewing thread cuts through the fold and because the sections cannot be held together by the glue. The glue peels off the back, bringing the surface of the paper with it and after very little use the leaves of the book become detached. The library binders are driven to guard with thin paper *every* fold in such books and even though this drastic operation is performed and the leaves are so strengthened in the fold that they can be securely held by the sewing thread the paper will tear and soil elsewhere.

This "woolly" paper is merely used to bulk out short books. The publishers say that this is necessary in order to sell the books. They may be right, but it seems foolish that books should be ruined in order to make them take up more room on the already overcrowded shelves in both public libraries and private houses. In this connection the recently issued report of the Library Association on the Durability of Paper should be studied.

While it is possible to have strong publishers' cases and good paper, in practice librarians have to deal with books that are flimsily bound and often are printed on worthless paper, and they have to decide whether they shall be re-bound and if so what kind of binding is best.

There are many books that will probably have little use, and these can generally be left as published if they are looked at from time to time when being returned to the shelves. Directly books begin to get floppy and the cases and plates show signs of getting loose the volume should be sent to the binders, as after this stage deterioration is very rapid.

All books in ordinary publishers' cloth cases which are expected to have hard wear should be re-bound before they are put into circulation. A few issues can be got out of the publisher's case, but a book already falling to pieces takes much longer to rebind than one that is in good condition.

For rebinding ordinary books the usual style of binding done by the regular library binders can hardly be bettered. The leaves of these books are first made sound in the fold where necessary and plates and single leaves are attached by guards. Endpapers are made with cloth joints that sometimes are folded round the first and last sections in heavy books. The books are sewn on not fewer than three tapes and the ends of these are held between double or "split" boards. For hard wear a narrow leather back is attached directly to the backs of the sections of small books, while very heavy, large books have an additional lining of leather under the cover.

The leather must be acid free, and goatskin, known as morocco, is the most serviceable leather in common use. Coloured pigskin is often unreliable, and sealskin, at one time highly recommended, has not in many cases proved to be very satisfactory. There is now some excellent English calf leather being made, but this is rather expensive, and the ordinary calf of the trade is worthless for much-used books.

The leather need not come far over on to the boards, but it must come far enough to be firmly fixed to them. The sides can be of any good cloth, and generally the cloth is best turned in at the corners without being cut. This makes rather clumsy-looking corners but adds to the wearing qualities of the binding. Alternatively, the corners of the board may be covered with vellum tips and the cloth cut so that the actual corner with the vellum is exposed. Vellum tips add a little to the cost of rebinding but they do help to harden the corners and avoid the unsightly ragged edges of worn cloth.

The boards for library binding should be good quality "medium" boards. Straw or pulp boards are too soft and too absorbent to be satisfactory. For books that will have occasional use only, a cover of good buckram will probably answer better than leather, but only if the inside work is done soundly. Unfortunately, it has become the custom to rather scamp the inside work on cloth-bound books.

Books bound singly have to be lettered by hand, generally with single letters. This is expensive and much time and cost can often be saved by reducing the amount of lettering to the least that will serve to identify the volume. Much unnecessary lettering can often be saved by the use of obvious contractions, especially on sets of books.

Many public libraries purchase a considerable proportion of their books direct from the library binders who buy large numbers of popular books second-hand from the great subscription libraries. These they rebind in lots and save much time by dealing with fairly large numbers of the same book at one time.

Librarians have to arrange for the binding of periodical literature, and binders should be asked to register the particulars of the binding of recurring periodicals and transactions so as to avoid the cost and trouble of sending a pattern volume with each binding order. In the case of periodical publications it is advisable to bind in the front covers either in place or together at the end of the volume, and sometimes advertisements or announcements are

BINDING FOR LIBRARIES

also preserved. This is a matter for the librarian, and the decision about what is to be bound in should not be left to the binder.

Sometimes pockets have to be provided to contain loose maps or plans. These should be attached to the inside of the back board, and of course should have the opening towards the joint. Guards to equal the thickness of the pocket and its contents should be provided.

Unusual books cannot as a rule be bound to any rigid specification. Generally the binder should be given a fairly free hand to deal with the special problems that such books present.

It is for the librarians to decide if the edges of books are to be cut or not. Generally it is advisable to cut the edges of books and especially of bound periodicals, as the sizes of the parts often vary; but the edges of books of value and of exceptional interest should not be cut or at most only cut at the head.

It is no use expecting the binder to discriminate between books that should have their edges cut and those that should be left uncut. In a library binding workshop books have to be treated in bulk and there is little time to examine them individually. Valuable books that require binding should be sent to a binder who specialises in this class of work and who will deal with books individually and with some appreciation and knowledge of their value.

Binding repairs are a constant worry to librarians who often find the appearance of their libraries sadly marred by rows of battered and disreputable volumes that perhaps have little present value. One way of dealing with such books is to cover them with buckram over the old bindings. There is a range of American library buckrams that are nearly the colour of old calf bindings, and if the lettering is made to range with the old volumes and there is some indication of the bands, re-covered volumes can take their place in sets without offence. Coloured labels can be added to the buckram backs to match the old volumes, but this adds considerably to the cost of re-covering. This system of covering can only be used where the sewing is sound. If the sewing is insecure the books must be re-bound.

Leather-bound books with perished backs or broken joints can be rebacked with new leather covering the spine and slipped under the leather of the sides. This requires some skill and dexterity to produce strong and neat results.

Although I have not attempted to deal with all aspects of binding in this short chapter and have not mentioned fine binding, librarians who respect books should always bear in mind that both printing and binding at its best may reach the standard of a minor work of art, and in every library I should like to see a permanent exhibition of specimens of finely printed and well-bound books. Such an exhibition would do much to form a standard of excellence for the production of books, and although the cheaper books cannot reach this high standard they may in their own class come near enough to it to be pleasant

BINDING FOR LIBRARIES

to handle and to read. In the long run the public will get the kind of book production that it wants, and librarians can do much to foster the appreciation of good work in paper, printing, and binding.

BINDING THAT CAN BE DONE BY THE LIBRARY STAFF

While it would not pay for any but the very largest libraries to bind the bulk of their books on the premises there are simple forms of binding that can be done by anyone who has had a little practice and has a few simple appliances.

I have written a series of four pamphlets dealing with "Bookbinding as a School Subject," and it has been pointed out that the instructions given in these pamphlets will serve the needs of librarians as well as school children. For instance, single-section pamphlets can be easily covered neatly and serviceably, and simple repairs can be managed by anyone who can paste neatly. Messrs. G. W. Russell & Son, of Hitchin, Herts, will supply the pamphlets and all the necessary appliances and materials.

BOOKS ON BINDING

COCKERELL. Bookbinding and the Care of Books. Pitman. 7s. 6d.
    Some Notes on Bookbinding. Oxford. 6s.
HEWITT BATES. Bookbinding for Schools. Dryad Handicrafts, Leicester. 6s.
VAUGHAN. Modern Bookbinding. Raithby, Lawrence & Co., Leicester. 12s. 6d.

CHAPTER XX

LIBRARY LAW

BY ALDERMAN J. S. PRITCHETT, M.A., J.P.
Hon. Legal Adviser to the Library Association

The earliest specimen of library legislation is to be found in the Parochial Libraries Act, 1708, being "An Act for the better Preservation of Parochial Libraries in that part of Great Britain called England." By it the care of parish libraries was vested in the incumbent of the parish with a duty imposed upon the Ordinary of enquiring into the state and condition of such libraries and amending and redressing grievances and defects. By this statute, which has never been repealed, the incumbent is empowered to bring an "Action of Trover and Conversion" against persons unlawfully removing or retaining a book, whereupon treble damages are to be given with full costs of suit and such damages applied to the use and benefit of the library. Every new incumbent was obliged to make a new catalogue within six months of his installation, to be signed by him and a copy sent to the Bishop. On a vacancy occurring in the incumbency the churchwardens were ordered immediately to lock up the library "to prevent the embezilment [*sic*] of the books until a new incumbent should be installed." Moreover, the Ordinary was empowered to make rules and orders for the better governing of the libraries and preserving the same, while it was lawful for any Justice of the Peace to grant a search warrant to search for any book missing. So far as it went this was an excellent piece of legislation and probably prevented the dispersal of many collections of books to which time has given great value.

Since 1708 there have been numerous Acts of Parliament (seventy-nine are enumerated in Hewitt's *Law relating to Public Libraries*) concerning libraries and books in one way or another, of which the most important is the Public Libraries Act, 1892, which made provision for the establishment of libraries in every urban district and parish not within an urban district. In an urban district the urban authority, i.e. the Council of the borough or urban district, was to be the library authority and in rural areas Commissioners appointed by the parish vestry. The Act was permissive and required adoption by a majority of the votes in the library district; moreover, it imposed a condition that the maximum rate for library purposes should not exceed one penny in the pound in any one financial year. This limitation to a penny rate seems ludicrous when we find that the library authority had power to provide public libraries and museums, schools of science, art galleries and schools of art and for that purpose to purchase land, erect buildings, and "fit up furnish and supply the same with all requisite furniture fittings and conveniences," not to mention the purchase of books. It was realised from the outset that the penny rate was absurd and a strong agitation was at once set on foot to remove the restriction, but, although several places succeeded in doing so by getting clauses inserted in private bills, it was not till 1919 that it was finally removed and the various localities permitted to spend what they thought fit. In this movement for freedom the Library Association played a prominent part, and it is largely through its influence that this much-needed reform was brought about. By the Public Libraries (Amendment) Act, 1893, power was given to an urban authority to adopt the Act without seeking the consent of the voters, and provision was made for neighbouring urban districts to combine for carrying the Act into operation. By the Local Government Act, 1894, the Libraries Act can be adopted by the parish meeting as constituted under that Act, and now by the Public Libraries Act, 1919, the County Council of any county in England or Wales has power by resolution specifying the area to which the resolution extends to adopt the Public Libraries Acts for the whole or any part of their county which is not an existing library area. As by this time nearly every county has resolved to adopt the Acts a library service may now be said to exist in every part of the country, supplemented and rendered still more effective by the establishment of the National Central Library. By the Public Libraries Act, 1901, which with the Acts of 1892 and 1893 may be cited as the Public Libraries Acts, 1892 to 1901, power was given to library authorities to make

LIBRARY LAW

bye-laws enforceable by penalties in courts of summary jurisdiction.

Finally, by the Public Libraries Act, 1919, already mentioned, any library authority being a local education authority is authorised to refer any matters relating to the exercise by them of their powers under the Public Libraries Acts to the Education Committee established under the Education Acts, and may delegate to that committee any of its powers other than that of raising a rate or borrowing money. So far as we are aware this power has not been exercised in any urban area, and it seems to be the general opinion that municipal libraries, at any rate, should continue to be managed by Library Committees separately from any Education Committee and directly responsible to the municipal council.

Library legislation has not left much room for litigation, and the law courts are now very seldom appealed to in connection with library matters. It should, however, be observed that a public library has been held to be a literary or scientific institution exempt from Income Tax whoever may be the owners of the building and whether supported by rates or not; on the other hand, public libraries are not exempt from the payment of rates, a point of no real importance, as the rates usually come out of one pocket into another. It remains only to mention the Libraries Offenders Act, 1898, which provides penalties for disorderly conduct in libraries, including refusal to quit at closing-time and a clause in the Public Health Acts Amendments Act, 1907, which prevents the use of library books by persons suffering from infectious disease.

It will be seen from the above that library law is permissive in character; the time may come when the establishment of libraries, like the provision of schools, becomes compulsory on the local authority everywhere; logically such should be the case if education is to be continued after leaving school and we are to become a really educated nation.

CHAPTER XXI

HOW TO ENTER THE LIBRARY PROFESSION

BY W. E. DOUBLEDAY, HON. F.L.A.
Chief Librarian of the Hampstead Public Libraries

Librarianship offers a reasonable prospect as a career for suitable persons, and is especially adapted for women; but it presents no sort of opening except for those who are specially trained for the work. A mere liking for books, admirable enough although that may be, is not by itself a passport to success, for modern librarianship demands technical knowledge, and the preparation for satisfactory service can be neither slight nor hurried. It is desirable that this preparation should be commenced at an early age, for, almost without exception, advertised appointments are either for junior assistants—whose qualifications will immediately be discussed—or for persons of approved experience in practical library work.

Senior library appointments are, generally speaking, offered only to candidates who have gained certificates at the professional examinations, and exceptions from this procedure are few and far between. Even in the case of beginners, at the foot of the lowest staff grade, where certificates cannot be produced a stipulation is apt to be made that the assistant shall enter for examination without undue

A PRIMER OF LIBRARIANSHIP

delay, and failure to pass that test may entail loss of position. Few libraries will promote from a lower into a higher grade where professional certificates have not been gained, and, in the School of Librarianship at least, there is a distinct tendency to make the official training a post-graduate course. Under existing conditions no candidates are permitted to sit at the examinations until they have passed the matriculation or some other[1] approved equivalent examination.

The examinations are conducted by the Library Association, which also organises Correspondence Courses and, in conjunction with the University of London, is responsible for the School of Librarianship at the University College, Gower Street, London. It further arranges for the education of students at the Extra-Mural Department of the University of Manchester, and provides Lecture Courses and Summer Schools at Birmingham, Glasgow, and Dublin.

The Correspondence Courses are conducted under the auspices of the Assistant Librarians' Section of the Library Association, and are open to candidates throughout the world. They are arranged in two series. The full course comprises twelve fortnightly lessons, extending each year from October to May. The subjects taken under the 1928 Syllabus are: (1) English Literary History;

---

[1] A list of these approved alternatives appears in the Syllabus of Examinations published by the Library Association, 26–27, Bedford Square, W.C.

HOW TO ENTER THE LIBRARY PROFESSION

(2) Elementary Bibliography and *either* Book Selection *or* Palæography and Archives; (3) Classification; (4) Cataloguing; (5) Library Organisation; and (6) Library Routine. Candidates undertaking these courses with a view of sitting at the examinations will find it necessary to do a fair amount of technical reading, as is prescribed by the respective tutors; they will also be called upon to write papers answering set questions. The examination may be taken in sections at different periods as the students may desire, and *pro tanto* certificates are awarded.

A supplementary Short Course, for revision only, is held annually during September and October, and consists of six fortnightly lessons with a test-paper. The fee for the full course is £1 1s. for members of the Library Association, and £2 2s. in the case of non-members. The fee for the Short Course is 10s. 6d. (£1 1s. for non-members). Applications for admission to the Longer Course must be received by October 10th, and for the Shorter Course by August 22nd. In each case it is requisite that the fee be remitted with the application, which should be addressed to the Hon. Sec., Correspondence Course (Mr. S. W. Martin), The Carnegie Library, Herne Hill Road, S.E.14.

New regulations are about to be introduced, and as and from 1933 the examinations will be divided into three parts: (1) Elementary; (2) Intermediate; and (3) Final. The first section will include the more elementary aspects of English Literary History, Classification, Cataloguing, Accession Methods, and Library Administration. The Intermediate Course is to be devoted exclusively to Classification and Cataloguing. Two papers are to be set in each of these subjects, and each examination will cover the whole course—subjects may not be taken at intervals. The Final Examination is to be divided into three parts: (1) English Literary History, with either the History of Science or the Literary History of Economics and Commerce as alternatives; (2) General Bibliography and Book Selection; and (3) Advanced Library Administration. Students are recommended to sit for these three parts at one examination, but it is possible to take them progressively, provided that the whole series is completed within two years. In addition, candidates must satisfy the examiners as to proficiency in two languages, one of which must be modern.

The examinations will continue to be held in May and December each year. Students who pass the Final thereby become entitled to receive the professional Diploma and may be elected to the Fellowship of the Association. Application for these distinctions should be made to the Secretary of the Library Association. Fellows are entitled to use the designation F.L.A. (Fellow of the Library Association), students upon passing the Intermediate Examination qualify for election as Associates, (Associate of the Library Association). The Library Association maintains a professional register of Fellows and Associates, and inclusion within this list is fast becoming regarded by Library Authori-

HOW TO ENTER THE LIBRARY PROFESSION

ties as a necessary qualification for appointment to library staffs.

The School of Librarianship provides oral tuition by special lectures, and is intended for such students as have had actual library experience or can devote the whole of their time to an extended and systematic course of study. Full-time students complete the course in two academic years; part-time students in not less than two years nor more than five. The curriculum is much the same as that of the Correspondence Courses, but with additional subjects. These additions include alternative languages, one of which must be either Greek, Latin, or Arabic, together with one of a number of approved modern languages. Special training in the organisation and routine methods of University, Business, and other non-municipal Libraries is also given, and Advanced Courses are arranged as required. There is also an Easter School, which is held yearly on the Continent. In connection with the School of Librarianship there is an Exhibition of £40 tenable for two years, the Director's Annual Prize, and the Sir John MacAlister Medal which is awarded annually to the student who shows the best results at the Diploma Examination. Candidates for admission to the School should apply to the Secretary, University College, Gower Street, W.C.1.

The Diploma with Honours is awarded to such holders of the Diploma of the Library Association as submit a satisfactory thesis showing research on some approved subject included within the scope of the curriculum. Diplomates of the School of Librarianship may obtain this Honours Diploma by submitting an original thesis of approved merit, and complying with the conditions as to library service. A list of the subjects already approved for these theses may be obtained upon application to the office of the Association. The regulation as to library service stipulates that no candidate can obtain a certificate for the Final Examination unless and until he (or she) has worked for not less than twenty-four hours a week for at least three years on the administrative staff of one or more libraries approved by the Association. It is possible for students to acquire this experience whilst preparing for their examinations. Many libraries accept part-time student-assistants and some pay them a more or less nominal salary.

For full details of all other library educational courses readers are referred to the official Syllabus of the Professional Examinations, issued by the Library Association. The price is 1s. (1s. 1d. post free). This guide, with its suggested courses of reading, is invaluable to all students in librarianship.

As a result of the Public Libraries Act, 1919, the position of rate-supported libraries has been greatly improved, owing to the fact that the restriction of the library rate was then abolished. The enlightened policy of the Carnegie United Kingdom Trustees has also forwarded the Library Movement considerably, with the result that there is now better payment of

HOW TO ENTER THE LIBRARY PROFESSION

library staffs, and, coincidentally, a larger number of appointments to be filled.

There is no national scale of salaries, and remuneration varies considerably, but most of the larger libraries have adopted staff grading schemes with scales of salaries, and frequently with contributory provision for superannuation. Assuming that "war bonus" has been incorporated in a consolidated salary, the remuneration of a junior Assistant may commence at anything from £65 to £100 *per annum*. A scale very generally in force in London provides for an initial salary of £75 for beginners of sixteen years of age, rising by annual increments of £15 to a maximum of £300. From this stage promotions are possible into higher grades at increased rates of pay. The second grade under this scheme commences at £315 and is augmented by annual increments of £15 to a maximum of £390. Deputy or Sub-Librarians receive a minimum salary of £405 which proceeds to a maximum of £500 by annual or biennial increments. Other scales may be higher or lower, but the trend is distinctly upward as the library service expands and a wider knowledge and a higher degree of technical competence are demanded of the staff. The salaries of Chief Librarians are not, and cannot be, standardised since they are contingent upon the scope of the library, the size and character of the library area, and other local circumstances. The largest libraries may pay a salary running into four figures, but the librarian of a small or medium-sized library may receive a salary appreciably less than that paid to a deputy librarian or other senior officer of a larger library system.

Superannuation schemes, municipal and other, differ in detail, but the general principle is that 5 per cent., or some other small proportion of salary, is in each instance deducted at the source of payment, the local Authority providing the balance to enable post-service annuities to be paid to the individuals concerned. Length of qualifying service determines the proportion to be paid. The usual scale reaches a maximum of two-thirds (generally described as forty-sixtieths) calculated on the average of the salary paid during the last five years of office. A shorter period of service naturally reduces the number of "fortieths" to be received, and a minimum of ten years has to be served before any superannuation can be claimed. There are provisions for the repayment of contributions in the event of termination of employment on account of ill-health, and for the "transfer of service" from one Authority to another. Retirement is compulsory at the age of sixty or sixty-five as the local regulations may decide.

Vacant librarianships and appointments of trained assistants are usually advertised in the *New Statesman and Nation*, the *Municipal Journal*, the *Local Government Journal*, *The Times*, and sometimes in the *Literary* and the *Educational Supplements* to that newspaper. It will also be worth while to keep an eye upon the advertisements in the official *Library Association Record*, and other professional journals.

INDEX

Accessioning, 92-4.
Acts of Parliament, 208-12.
Administrative departments, 60.
Aids to readers, 95-103.
Annotations, 60, 186-7.
Anonymous works, 52
Appointments, library, 213-14, 220.
Architecture, library, 62-3.
Atlases, library use of, 163-4, 175.
Author-catalogues, 53
Author-entries, 47.

B.B.C. and libraries, 140-1.
Bespoke books, 89.
Bibliographical terms, 20-5.
Bibliographies, 15; of subjects, 14, 27.
Bibliography, 11-25; term defined, 11, 13
Binding, cased books, 200-2; reinforced, 200-1; paper difficulties, 201-2; library binding methods, 202-3; materials, 203-4; covers, 204; finishing processes, 204; special requirements, 205; cut edges, 205; buckram coverings, 206; leathers, 203, 206; fine bindings, 206-7; *Bookbinding as a School Subject*, 207; books about binding, 207.
Blind, embossed books for the, 143-4.
Block books, 20.
Book—classification, 34-44; displays, 99-102; illustration, 17, 19; imprints, 23, 50; lists, 101-3; production, 16; purchasing, 120; reviews discussed, 30-1; selection, 26-33, 120; stacks, 64; stock percentages, 28-9; storage schemes, 63-4.
Books, children's, 108; reference, 65.
Borrowers' application forms, 70; registration methods, 70-1, 80-1, 82-5; tickets, 71-2, 82-5.
Branch libraries, 148-9.
Buckram, use of, 206.
Budgets, library, 117.
Bulletins, library, 190-1.
Business libraries, 174-82; their scope and purpose, 174; periodicals and their treatment in, 175; routine methods, 176-8; filing, 178-9; catalogues of, 179-81; cost of, 181-2; staff of, 182.
Bye-laws, library, 210-11.

Cased books, 200-1, 202.
Catalogues, nature and purpose of, 45-6; 77, 134; for children, 185; for county libraries, 145, 150; union catalogues, 154-5; university library, 134; varieties of, 184 *et seq*.
Cataloguing, 45-58; Anglo-American rules, 51-2; Cutter's rules, 45; consistency in, 50; departments for, 60; forms of, 53-4; entry, forms of, in, 46-55; annotations in, 50; subject-indexes to, 53, 57; subject-headings, 55-7.
Charging methods, 72, 79, 85-7, 146-7.

Children's libraries, 104-12; history of, 104; increase of, 104-5; structural needs, 105; varieties of, 106-7; fittings for, 107-8; book-stock for, 108; hours of opening, 108; rules for, 109; extension services, 109-10; picture collections in, 110; magazines in, 111; school co-operation with, 111, staff and training for, 111-12; catalogues for, 185.
Cinematograph lectures, 141-2.
Classification of books, 34-44; classification defined, 34; varieties of, 34; characteristics in, 35-6; Tree of Porphyry, 36-8; *natural* and *artificial*, 38; essentials in, 42; difficulties of, 42-3; university methods of, 134.
Classified catalogues, 54, 58.
Clippings, treatment of, 178-81.
Cloth-bound books, 200-1, 202.
Collation, 21, 48-50.
Commercial and technical libraries, 67, 161-73; purpose of, 161; organisation of 161-2; book-stock of, 162-3; other material, 162-3; access by readers in, 163; catalogues in, 163; classification in, 163; atlases and maps in, 163-4; use of periodicals in, 164-6; trade catalogues in, 164; display racks in, 165; filing work in, 166; routine work of, 166; special indexes in, 167; other special features, 168-70; main uses of, 171-3.
Committees, Public Library, powers of, 113; methods, 114; delegated powers of, 115-16; control of, 115; procedure of, 115; minutes and reports of, 116, 121; finance, 117; Council supervision of, 117-18; book selection and purchase by, 120; statistical returns for, 122; sub-committees, 122; University, 131.
Co-operation, library, 68-137; county library, 151; regional schemes of, 153-6; outlier libraries and, 157-8. *See also* National Central Library.
Correspondence training courses, 214.
Correspondence, treatment of, 123-6.
County libraries, books on, 145; books and their preparation for, 145; cataloguing in, 145-6; headquarters routine work, 145-7, 148; book-charging in, 146-7; local centres, 147; distribution problems, 147-51; delivery and exhibition vans, 148-50; publicity methods for, 150; talks in, 150; catalogues and handlists in, 150-1; co-operation between, 151; educational recognition of, 151; probable developments of, 152.
Cutter's Cataloguing rules, 45.

Delivery vans, library, 149.
Departmental libraries, 135.
Dictionary catalogues, 54.

221

Diploma of the Library Association, 216, 217-18.
Durability of paper, 202.

Edition, term defined, 22.
Education Committees, 211.
Education, libraries and, 151.
Engravings, processes of, 195; prints and "proofs," varieties of, 195-6; pitfalls and tests, 196-7; classification of, 197, 199; catalogues of, 197-8; storage and preservation of, 197-8; books about, 198-9, indexing, 199.
Enquiry desks, 74.
Enquiry registers, 33, 98.
Epidiascopes, 68, 141.
Estimates, library, 117.
Examinations, library, 213-18.
Exhibitions, book, 99-102, 149; other, 142-3.
Extension work, library, objects, 68, 138; lectures, 138-40; B.B.C. listening groups, 140-1; cinematograph work, 141-2; story-hours, 142; exhibitions, 142-3; holiday bureaux, 143; co-operation with Societies, 143; books for the blind, 143-4; hospital libraries, 144; Seafarers' Education Service, 144.

Faked engravings, 197.
Film lectures, 141-2.
Finance, library, municipal, 117; university, 131.
Fines and receipts, 88.
Furniture and fittings, 64.

Galley, a printing term, 23.
Glasgow Library classified catalogue, 54.
Glossary of terms, 20-5.
Gramophones and libraries, 64, 139, 140-1.
Guidance for readers, 75.
Guildhall Library, London, 192, 197.

Historical fiction guides, 27.
Holiday bureaux, 143.
Hospital libraries, 144.

Illustration, book, 17, 19.
Imposition, printing term, 23.
Imprints, 23, 50.
Income tax, library, 211.
Indexes for commercial libraries, 167.
Indexing, F. H. Collins, on, 16.
Infection, 89-90, 212.
Information bureaux, 174.
Inter-library loans, 91.
Issues of books, 77.

Justification, printing term, 24.

Law, library, history of, 208-10; Acts of Parliament, 210; Public Libraries Act (1919), 211; income tax exemption, 211; liability for rates, 211; Library Offenders Act (1898), 211; Public Health Acts Amendment Act (1907), 212.
Leading, printing term, 24.
Leather for bindings, 19-20, 203, 206.
Lectures, library, 68; for children, 109-10; University Extension courses, 139; music, 139-40; cinematographs and, 141-2; legal aspect of, 142.

Leeds Public Library handbooks, 27.
Leeds University Library, 136.
Legislation, library, 208-12.
Lending libraries, 70-77; structural characteristics, 70; administration of, 70; borrowers, 71-2, 80-5; tickets, 72, 82-5; 85-6; book-charging in, 72; regulations for, 72-3; mechanical aids for readers, 73-4, 95-7; enquiry desks, 74; Shelf orderliness in, 75; statistics of, 77; routine work of, 78-94; registration of borrowers in, 71-2, 80-3; lost tickets, 85, discharging books in, 87; book renewals in, 87-8; overdues, 88; Fine and receipts, 87-8; bespoke books in, 89; infection checks, 89-90, 212; statistical returns of, 90-1; inter-library loans, 91; taking stock in, 91-2; accessioning, 92-4; order-forms and checking for, 92-4; process stamps, 93.
Libraries Acts, 104, 208-12.
Libraries, business, 174-82; children's, 104-12; commercial and technical, 161-73; county and rural, 145-52; lending, 70-94; reference, 59-69; University, 127-37.
Library extension work, see Extension work.
Library planning, 62-3.
Loans between libraries, 91, 153-60.
Local Government Act (1894), 210.
London, library co-operation in, 156; topographical views of, 194-5.
Lost tickets, 85.

Magazines, library, 111.
Manuals of bibliography, 15.
Maps, use of, 163, 175.
Metal book-stacks, 64.
Mezzotints, 196.
Minutes, committee, 116.
Music in libraries, 64.
Music lectures, 139-40.

National Central Library, 31, 32, 68, 96, 137, 151; and regional co-operation, 153-60; its union catalogue, 154-5; provincial co-operation, 156; its outlier libraries, 157-8; its functions, 157-8.

Offenders Act (1898), 211.
Office routine, 122-3.
Open-access, 134-5.
Order-forms, book, 120-1.
Ordering and checking-off, 92-4.
Organisation, office, 122-3.
Outlier libraries, 157-158.
Overdue books, 88.

Pamphlets, 178-81.
Paper, making, 17, 21; strength of, 201; "woolly," 201; inferior, 201; Durability of Paper Report, 202.
Parliamentary papers, 47.
Patent specifications, 165.
Periodicals, binding of, 204; in business libraries, 177-8; in commercial libraries, 165-8; supply of, 133-4; library, 190-1.
Photographic collections, 193.
Picture cleaning, 199.
Picture collections, 110.
Planning of libraries, 62-3.

INDEX

Porphyry, Tree of, 36–8.
Posters, library, 191.
Prefixes in cataloguing, 51.
Print collecting, 192–9; restoration, 199.
Printing, books on, 15, 16, 19; catalogue, 187; mediaeval, 12; papers for, 17; terms defined, 17, 20–5.
Process stamps, 93.
Proof correcting, 16.
Proportional stock, 28–9.
Pseudonymous works, 52.
Public Libraries Report (1927), 153.
Publications, library, 111; their purpose, 183–4; catalogues, 184–5; children's catalogues, 185; reading lists, 185–6, 189; annotations, 186; graded lists, 186–7; specialist co-operation in preparing, 187–8; distribution of, 188; topical lists, 188–9; magazines and bulletins, 190–1; posters, 191.
Publicity, library, 150; 183–91.
Publisher's cloth, 200–1.
Purchase of books, 120.

Rates, liability for, 211.
Readers' suggestions, 32.
Reading-lists, 103.
Reference libraries, 59–69; scope of, 59; special libraries, 59–60; routine work in, 60–1, 65–6; planning of, 62–3; book storage for, 63–4; gramophone rooms, 64; metal stacks in, 64; furniture in, 64; books for, 65; home-reading, use of, 66; commercial, 67, 161–73; special collections in, 67; co-operative work between, 68; extension work in, 68.
Regional co-operation, 153–60.
Registers, library, 83–5.
Registration of borrowers, 70–1, 80–1.
Regulations, public, 72–3; staff, 79.
Renewing books, 87–8.
Reports of committees, 116, 121.
Reviews, book, 30–1.
Rural libraries, 147.

Salaries, library, 219–20.
School libraries, 111.
School of Librarianship, 217.
Second-hand books, 30.
Seminar libraries, 136.
Shelf arrangement, 73–5, 78, 80.
Shelf-registers, 91–2.
Shipping information, 172.
Signatures, typographical, 25.
Sizes of books, 48–9.
Societies, co-operation with, 143.
Societies, publications of, 47, 51.
Special collections, 135.
Special libraries, 59–60, 67.
Stacks, metal, 64.
Staff grading, 213–14; regulations, 79; reports, 121; salaries, 219–20; training, 112, 131, 213–18; work-books, 79.

Statistics, library, 77, 122.
Story-hours, 108–10, 142.
Sub-Committees, 123.
Subject-entries, 55; headings, 55–7; indexes, 53, 57.
Suggestions, readers', 90.
Superannuation, 220.

Talks on books, 150; *see also* Lectures.
Tariffs, 168.
Technical libraries, *see* Business libraries and Commercial libraries.
Terms, technical, 20–5.
Theatre-bills, 199.
Tickets, borrowers', 72, 82–5; 146–7.
Title-entries, 47–8.
Title-pages, early, 12–13.
Topical lists, 188.
Topographical collections, 194–5.
Trade catalogues, 164, 175; periodicals, 165.
Training, library, 112, 131, 213–18.
Transactions of Societies, 47.
Tree of Porphyry, 36–8.
Type, early founts, 12.
Type for catalogues, 187.
Typewriting, 124.
Typographical terms, 17, 20–5.

Union catalogues, London, 156, 158; national, 154, 158.
University College, London, 217.
University Extension Lectures, 139.
University libraries, co-operation between, 68, 137; administration of, 127; staffs of, 130–1; book selection for, 131; finances of, 131; periodicals in, 131, 133–4; catalogues in, 134; access by readers in, 134; special collections, 135; departmental libraries, 135; seminar libraries, 136; registers used in, 136–7; inter-library loans, 137.

Vans, library, 149.
Vellum tips, 203.
Ventilation, 64.
Vertical files, 178–9, 181–2.
Vouchers, application, 80–2.

Wales, regional co-operation in, 155–6.
Warwickshire regional co-operation, 155.
West Midland Regional Bureau, 155.
Westmoreland regional co-operation, 154.
Wire lines defined, 21.
Wireless listening groups, 140–1.
Work-books, staff, 79.
Workers' Educational Association groups, 151.
Works libraries, 174–82.
Wyer, J. I. *Reference Work*, 61, 68.

223

For Product Safety Concerns and Information please contact our EU
representative GPSR@taylorandfrancis.com
Taylor & Francis Verlag GmbH, Kaufingerstraße 24, 80331 München, Germany

www.ingramcontent.com/pod-product-compliance
Lightning Source LLC
Chambersburg PA
CBHW062223300426
44115CB00012BA/2194